Praise for *Love the Journey to College*

"Jill Madenberg draws on her extensive experience as a college counselor to create one of the best books on how to get into college that I have read. But this is not just another admissions how-to book. Jill and her daughter Amanda offer advice, wisdom, and a uniquely candid and personal window into how students and parents intersect in the college admissions journey. My hat's off to the authors for creating a book which is readable, strategic, and sane!"

–WILLIAM SHAIN, *Fmr. Dean of Admissions, Vanderbilt University and Bowdoin and Macalester Colleges; Fmr. Regional Director of Admissions, Princeton University*

"Preparing for college is a daunting task filled with myriad tough questions and hard decisions. Jill and Amanda Madenberg's *Love the Journey to College* is an effective tool that will help high school students make wise choices early in the process so the journey is successful and enjoyable. A wonderful read, and I highly recommend it."

–DAN DOMENECH, *Executive Director, American Association of School Administrators (AASA)*

"I love this book! I honestly think it's the best example on the market of clear, factual information and great common sense advice that works for both parent and applicant. I am frequently asked for advice about the college process, and I will recommend *Love the Journey to College* to everyone I know."

–MARILEE JONES, *Fmr. Dean of Admissions, MIT*

"*Love the Journey to College* is a comprehensive, readable, and engaging discussion of what can be a complex process known as college admissions. Jill Madenberg's experience as a guidance counselor and college consultant provides an expertise and breadth of knowledge that are invaluable as she discusses the full range of issues involved in preparing for, applying to and enrolling in college. Amanda's very recent, lived experience as the student going through the journey adds a dimension to the process that is honest, fresh, and enlightening. This book is a great resource for parents and students, starting as early as ninth grade and all the way through until freshman year."

–SUSAN H. MURPHY, *PhD, Vice President Emerita and former Dean of Admissions and Financial Aid, Cornell University*

"This book is a 'must-read' for parents, students, school counselors, and anyone else interested in college admissions. It is chock-full of useful information and very helpful answers to FAQs."

–Lisa Suzuki, *Ph.D. Associate Professor Counseling Psychology, New York University*

W9-CHH-984

"As a long-time admissions professional in New England, I highly recommend this book for understanding the admission process from the student's, family's, and admission officer's perspectives. *Love the Journey to College* is informative about every aspect of the college journey, and Jill and Amanda's joint writing style is truly special. One key bit of advice they provide: be joyful in the search!"

–WILLIAM DUNFEY, *Executive Director of Admissions at Massachusetts College of Pharmacy and Health Sciences*

"Jill and Amanda Madenberg capture the process of applying to college from start to finish. Jill's wisdom as a mother, an experienced counselor, and knowledgeable communicator, plus Amanda's personal and thoughtful insights as a daughter and high school student are a winning combination. The mother/daughter 'hook' makes this valuable book an easy read for students, parents, and educators!"

–LORETTA NUGENT, *Principal, New Hyde Park Memorial High School, New Hyde Park, NY (Ret.)*

"Jill Madenberg's book is a perfect illustration of her care and thoughtfulness in helping families navigate "the journey to college." The process is laden with anxiety and pressure, and it is a breath of fresh air to work with Jill, who consistently brings calmness to her clients. She has been a trusted and respected resource for us, and we are grateful for Jill's extensive experience, deep knowledge, and her dedication to providing holistic support for students—a commitment we share."

–JEREMY COHEN, *Partner, Private Prep, Long Island, NY*

"From my perspective in the field of university student life, *Love the Journey to College* is a must-read for parents and students considering college. Jill and Amanda take what can be a stressful process and provide tools for staying healthy throughout and coming out satisfied on the other side. This book's expert and personal advice will help you manage emotions, maintain composure, and evaluate options as the college decisions arrive. The process only happens once, so enjoy the journey!"

–RICHARD WOLCOTT, *Director of Conference Services, St. John's University; Fmr. Assistant Dean of Students, Seton Hall University*

"Jill and Amanda Madenberg have written a clear, comprehensive, highly readable guide through the often maze-like college process. It is replete with common sense and demystifies what must be done. Each step from the selection of colleges through completing the actual applications is laid out very clearly. This book will assist in minimizing student anxiety and in lowering parental blood pressure."

–ALICE D'ADDARIO, *Department Chair, Social Studies, Walt Whitman HS, South Huntington, NY (Ret.), Independent College Counselor*

"Jill and Amanda Madenberg have collaborated on a remarkably readable introduction to college admissions. It is based on Jill's two decades of experience as both a school counselor and independent educational consultant and draws on knowledge gained through the very personal journey through the process with her daughter. This book is chock-full of useful and up-to-date information provided with a great deal of motherly reassurance and encouragement. And the advice for high school students caught-up in the process to 'be authentically you' is a message we can all take to heart."

–NANCY GRIESEMER, *Independent Educational Consultant*

"After reading this book, my parents and I have a game plan for getting into the college of my dreams. I especially liked the detailed tips and tricks that Amanda shared. Now I know what to expect!"

–DEMETRIUS, *a High School Junior*

"I wish I had read this book before I started applying to colleges!"

–EVERLY, *a High School Senior*

"I'm in ninth grade and I have so many questions about high school and college. This will be my go-to-guide for all of it."

–SASHA, *a High School Freshman*

"This book really helped our family to take a calm, deliberate and informed approach to college acceptance. Now I feel like I know how to help my son through the process, rather than trying to drag him through it. There is so much to know, that it was overwhelming. But, thanks to the expert advice from Jill and the real-life insight from Amanda, we are much more confident about the whole 'journey!'"

–PATRICIA AND MURRAY, *Parents of a High School Senior*

"I would recommend this book to every student preparing for college, and to every parent who wants to help make the process as easy and smooth as possible. Jill and Amanda really help take the pressure off by giving you what you need to know about getting into the college of your choice."

–SUSAN, *Parent of a High School Senior*

LOVE
THE
JOURNEY TO
COLLEGE

Guidance from an Admissions Consultant and Her Daughter

Jill Madenberg
MA Counseling & Guidance, HECA, NACAC,
Associate Member IECA

Amanda Madenberg

A POST HILL PRESS BOOK

Love the Journey to College:
Guidance from an Admissions Consultant and Her Daughter
© 2017 by Jill Madenberg and Amanda Madenberg
All Rights Reserved

ISBN: 978-1-68261-349-8
ISBN (eBook): 978-1-68261-350-4

Interior Design and Composition by Greg Johnson/Textbook Perfect

Post Hill Press
New York • Nashville
posthillpress.com

Published in the United States of America

DISCLAIMER

In this book, we frequently mention students who have encountered certain situations as they applied to college. We have taken care to change some details in each story to protect the identities of these clients and friends.

DEDICATION

To Doug and Eric, for their love and support
and for being the point of it all.

TABLE OF CONTENTS

Part III Mental Health

ACKNOWLEDGMENTS

Our first thank you goes to Peter Tamburello, editor extraordinaire. Your suggestions and insights have been invaluable.

To our indefatigable marketing team: you have made this possible. Karen West, you run our ship effortlessly and we thank you for all your hard work. Melissa Gibson and Sherry Harnick, thank you for the public relations, marketing, promotion, and editing ideas. Amanda and I are grateful to KJAMS for your love, friendship, and guidance. As an advisor to our team, thank you to Jeanne Ellinport for your support and suggestions.

Thank you to our entire family for your love and support. In particular, a big thank you to Doug Madenberg and Judy Madenberg for providing your thoughts and for cheering us along the way.

We are blessed to live in the wonderful district of Great Neck Public Schools. We thank Amanda's phenomenal teachers and her high school counselor, Carly Bank. A special thank you to South High's English department, especially Jennifer Hastings, for fostering Amanda's love of writing.

The foundation provided by Amanda's early teachers played a major role in her development and love of learning. Hugs and thank yous to Marilyn Thabet, Barbara Raber, Robin Levine, Shelly Stern, Linda Ullman, and Kerry Spatz.

For academic and overall support, we thank Jeremy Cohen, Michael Cerro, and Miyuki Miyagi. Beyond the classroom, Stephanie Rosen, Tracy Grossman, and Jennifer Mitgang gave us support and enabled Jill to be the best mom she could be.

As a new school guidance counselor, Jill worked with amazing colleagues and administrators at New Hyde Park Memorial High School and the Sewanhaka Central High School District, who saw the value of encouraging students to visit and pursue colleges beyond Long Island. Thanks to Gerard Connors, Michael DeMartino, Thomas Dolan, and Loretta Nugent, who all had faith in Jill from the start.

In the world of education and college counseling, Jill is thankful to be supported by so many colleagues. Marilee Jones has become a trusted friend and resource to both Jill and Amanda. Jed Applerouth, Alice D'Addario, William Dunfey, Nancy Griesemer, Adam Ingersoll, Patrick O'Connor, William Shain, and Cigus Vanni generously share their knowledge freely. And a heartfelt note of appreciation to Loretta, Nancy, and Bill for the valuable suggestions for this book.

The road to having this book published began with Risa Beckett and Carol Frank; we are so grateful for your help. And of course, thank you to Anthony Ziccardi, Billie Brownell, and the Post Hill Press team.

INTRODUCTION

From Jill Madenberg

More often than not, people contact me in a mild state of panic. "My daughter is a high school junior and we have no idea what to do about college." "Should my son stay in his AP class and get Bs or go into a regular class and get As?" "My daughter bombed the SAT three times; should we try again or jump to the ACT?"

When students enter high school, it does not take long for them to start thinking about college. Which courses should I take? Am I getting involved in the right activities? Will I have the grades and test scores to be *Accepted* at College X? Students hear things about the college process—some accurate and some not—from their teachers, friends, counselors, and parents, and this often results in a growing sense of pressure and stress about their unknown future. Unfortunately, this anxiety among students and their parents can spoil a process that can (and should) be an exciting, eye-opening, and wonderful one.

In almost 25 years of experience as a high school guidance counselor, a college admissions staff member, and a private college counselor, I have noted the kinds of things that make the college process productive, successful, and enjoyable. While it can be a daunting and challenging process, it does not need to be too scary or overly stressful. I have worked with so many students who have blossomed in part due to their college search and application process. It can be a period of maturation and of self-exploration, with an honest assessment of skills and interests, development of task organization and discipline, renewed intrafamily communication, and travel to interesting cities and small college towns. I firmly believe when the journey to college is fully embraced, it can truly be loved.

The idea of writing this book actually came from the student with whom I had the most fun and meaningful college search and application experience; the one for whom all of my prior knowledge and experience crystalized into the most amazing journey—my daughter, Amanda. When she said, "Mom, we should write a book about this," I never doubted that she had the ability, creativity, and tenacity to make this project a reality. On the pages that follow, as I give advice about the various aspects of the process, Amanda comments throughout and shares her own perspective as a student and daughter. Our intention with this joint format is to provide a useful guide both for parents and students.

We are so excited to share our tips and strategies, our attitudes and experiences, with the hope that they will help calm your nerves and help you enjoy your journey as much as we enjoyed ours.

From Amanda Madenberg

From the moment I walked into high school, I was surrounded by college-talk—fueled by teachers, coaches, friends, and peers. It can actually be pretty easy to fall into the trap: getting wrapped up in rumors, grade-sharing, and the competitive outlook that can permeate student life. It was not until I matured throughout the past few years that I was able to (almost fully) accept the occasional low test grade and recognize what I could do to manage my own stress regarding college admissions.

Of course, college-talk has been a part of my own life for as long as I can remember. Professionally, my mom is an Independent

Educational Consultant, which means she helps students with the college process. I've always enjoyed watching my mom in action. When I was a little girl, I would sit in her office when she met with the "big kids" and helped them with essays and applications. She spends hours making lists of potential schools for each client, she talks and Skypes with them about what classes to take, or why they should ask one teacher over another for a letter of recommendation, or why they should consider a certain school again. A huge (and fun) aspect of being the daughter of a college counselor were the many college visits I took even prior to high school. Family road trips have always included stops at one or two colleges on the way. I loved to watch my mom approach college students and ask them about their experiences, come back to the car, and explain how wonderful the campus personality is.

However, it wasn't until my own college journey that I could fully appreciate my mom's approach to the application process: an emphasis on the journey—not the destination. My mom tackles her job with a smile, a breath of fresh air, and love. She has helped hundreds of families conquer an experience that they will remember for the rest of their lives, and she often becomes so deeply invested in those students that they keep in touch years later. I so greatly admire her dedication and passion to her work, and hope that one day I will love my professional field half as much as she does.

I've always loved to write. When I was in elementary school and first learned to write memoirs, I found that I loved sharing stories through words with others. Naturally, a dream I have always had is to write a book. During my senior year of high school, I was reflecting on my college process and how much I was going to miss it (weird as it sounds). So, I asked my mom if we could write a book on the process in an attempt to help other people have similar experiences. I hope you find my mom as helpful and this process as enjoyable as I did. Good luck!

HOW TO USE THIS BOOK

With both Jill and Amanda as cowriters of this book, we've used the initials $\mathcal{J}$ and $\mathbf{A}$ to distinguish who is the chapter author and who is commenting within the chapter. A chapter that opens with a $\mathcal{J}$ at the top is written by Jill, and the comments within the chapter that appear in a different font and have the letter $\mathbf{A}$ are made by Amanda. In a few of the chapters, the roles are reversed.

Below are examples of text and comments from the book. We used a straight or wavy underline to connect the text to its corresponding comment. We alternated between the two to enable a reader to identify the related text and comments quickly.

> You are most likely familiar with the braggers. These are the people who deliberately *go out of their way* to share their average and scores with you, and after doing so, <u>will ask to hear how you did</u>.
>
> $\mathcal{J}$ And you should know that <u>sometimes they are not telling you the truth</u> anyway.

> Consider your <u>favorite subjects</u>. With which classes do you want to spend the most time? Students often prefer math and science over social studies and English, or vice versa.
>
> I'm an "<u>English person</u>," but I wasn't afraid to challenge myself with math classes. However, especially as I've gotten older and have had more freedom to play around with my schedule a bit, I have tried to take more English classes and electives. I was able to take AP English, advanced journalism, and creative writing during my senior year.

PART I

HIGH SCHOOL RÉSUMÉ

CHAPTER 1

Knowing Where and When to Start

For better or for worse, we live in a society that emphasizes not only the importance of a college education, but also the start of this process at a young age. Even if you are only on the verge of entering high school, you probably have a little bit of college on the brain. How many times have you heard an older sibling, cousin or friend tell you that they did something in high school for no other reason than to have a better chance at getting into <u>college</u>?

> **A** Personally, it makes me so mad to hear people say that they are only participating in something because "it looks good for <u>college</u>." I have always stayed true to myself and my interests in high school and have only done things that I want to do for me. If an activity or a class happens to "look good" for college, I think that's a bonus.

The reality is that your grades start to matter the minute you take your first high school <u>class</u>. Although some colleges will not consider your freshman year grades when calculating your grade point average, many colleges will use them. The other reality? Colleges really like to see that you have stuck with the same extra-curricular activities throughout high school.

When I took high school-level Earth Science and Algebra in eighth grade, I don't think I was able to fully grasp this concept. However, it's important to try your best in these classes, even if you take them in middle school. It only helps your grade point average to do well in these relatively easier high school classes while your workload still is not crazy.

When you think about it, that is a lot of pressure for a 14-year-old. *The grades you get and the clubs you join as a freshman will matter when you apply to college?* However, this is not the whole story: if you live your life worrying about college, your high school years will slip past you.

I once had a student who had always been super athletic, and played three competitive sports up through ninth grade. When he was unexpectedly injured that year, he worried for a moment about what he was going to do: his life had revolved around sports. Ironically, his obstacle actually opened doors for him (as many obstacles eventually do). He developed a tremendous interest in firefighting and helping people escape emergency situations, and as a result became more and more involved in his local fire department. By his senior year of high school, firefighting had become his biggest commitment, the highlight of his school career, and the topic of his college essay. Because of this student's athletic injury, he found himself involved in another meaningful activity, something that happens to students all the time. Don't focus so much on what you think colleges will want to see; try to engage with activities that really mean something to you. Before you know it, you will be a senior with your very own story to tell colleges. There is so much time for growth, development, and change throughout high school, and colleges understand that.

As clichéd as it may sound, try to let high school work itself out. Don't overanalyze every move you make starting in ninth grade—you will drive yourself (and people around you) crazy. When you enter high school, just be yourself. Take the classes that interest you and join the clubs that align with what you see yourself doing during your free time. Live in the moment and take advantage of what your school has to offer, but don't become set on one particular path; you never know what can happen!

A common misconception exists that there are certain extra-curricular activities that colleges "like," and that this should be the driving factor behind your choice of activities. This is absolutely not true.

> Although some clubs and activities are considered more academic and challenging than others, what's important is your contributions to the activities you select. I really believe this because when completing a college application, the important thing is how you explain your commitment, not what the organization or activity is officially called. I had an easier time on the Common App with the activities I was most passionate about because it was evident that I had wanted to help the club.

Especially in ninth and tenth grades, do yourself a huge favor and just don't worry about college. Join clubs that are authentically you. Do things for your own sake, not for the sole purpose of getting *Accepted* to your dream school. Students also mistakenly believe that if they become involved in all the "right" activities and take the hardest classes, they have written their tickets to any school in the country. Unfortunately, college admissions do not work like that. Your admission to any given school is based on so many factors that it is almost impossible to calculate your chances at that school (see Chapter 11 on *Recognizing College Criteria*). Because there is no guarantee, do not end your high school career wishing you had done something differently. Spend your precious time the way you want to spend it, and college will work itself out. The beauty of having *Likely Schools* (see Chapter 10 on *Making a College List*) is the reassurance that you will most likely be *Accepted* to several schools, regardless of your activities.

Eventually, there comes a time in high school when it is appropriate to start thinking about college, not *obsessing*, but thinking about it. For example, students in grades 10 or 11 may want to think about how they learn best and what social situations bring out the best in them. They also may want to consider taking SAT subject tests in May or June of their sophomore year, especially after completing an Honors or AP course. With the help of review books and other resources, a few high scores checked off your list during 10th grade will make the end of junior year less stressful.

A Tell me about it. Although I attempted one subject test at the end of my sophomore year, it essentially did not matter because the score was not one I considered sending to colleges. However, if you work hard enough, the tests are manageable. I was really in over my head by the end of junior year when I attempted three more subject tests.

For students who prefer to get ahead with standardized testing, it is probably also helpful to map out a test schedule before grade 11. Secure SAT and ACT dates for your calendar and register as soon as you know you are taking a test. Staying proactive will help you manage your stress, especially during junior year.

A Although I did not take my first ACT until December of my junior year, I found it helpful to make a plan earlier. I took diagnostic SAT and ACT tests during Spring Break of 10th grade. I highly recommend this because you'll be able to see which test you prefer without the pressure of junior year.

It is super helpful to begin your college visits as early as freshman or sophomore year. This way, you can look at the schools without any pressure and determine what characteristics you like and do not (see Chapter 9 on *Visiting Colleges*). For example, can you see yourself more at a big school? Small school? City school? School with a campus? I recommend visiting at least three schools that *you do not think you will apply to*. Visiting early will significantly help you when making a college list in the future and in developing criteria for choosing a college.

Once you feel that high school has become "higher stakes"—for most students, this occurs during junior year—it becomes especially important for you to keep yourself physically and mentally healthy. Make the most of time not only spent on your studies, but also on extracurriculars, sleep, meals, and even car rides. When you are studying, focus. When you are not studying, enjoy the time with family and friends.

> **A** This is so important. As essential as it is to study, it's equally as essential deliberately *not* to study. Enjoy even those few minutes in the car ride to your soccer game or your family dinner because those are moments when you can relax and let your mind wander.

It is essential to eat well and exercise regularly if at all possible. While your schoolwork will keep you busy, you need the mental and psychological stability to support your studies. You also need sleep. Eight to ten hours is the recommended number for adolescents. I often told Amanda that if her schoolwork required too many hours, she would need to cut back on the Honors and AP classes; sleep is more important.

> **A** Ok, let's be real: hardly anyone in high school is sleeping for this long. However, I always found a way to get into bed at a reasonable hour, despite my busy schedule. I don't know about you, but I don't typically do well in school when I am groggy and tired. It's important to get the sleep you need.

You will have to think about college a lot throughout junior and senior years when you are making your list and applying. However, this is entirely possible without driving yourself crazy. Manage your time well during freshman and sophomore years and do not obsess about which college you will attend. Focus on being a good student, getting involved, and making the most of your high school experience. Remember that college will work itself out and you are in high school to actually *be in high school*! Enjoy it—there are plenty of meaningful experiences waiting for you if you seek them out.

A As I reflect on my high school experience this semester before I graduate, I think about all the highlights. I have participated in amazing programs within my school, and they are all things that I authentically enjoy. I've also had my fair share of engaging classes, despite subject matter that is not my favorite.

CHAPTER 2

Choosing High School Classes

In my nearly 25 years as a counselor, the number one question I have been asked is if it's better to get an "A" in a regular class or a "B" in an Honors/AP class. The answer? Top-tier colleges ideally want to see As in the most challenging classes. However, my general rule of thumb is that if you can get an 85 or better without sacrificing too much sleep or being too overwhelmed, you should take the more rigorous class.

That said, choosing your course load each year is extremely important. Your teachers can impact your grades positively or negatively, and you can end up with just one class that inspires you in a certain subject area. Your <u>classes</u> roughly determine the amount of time you will need to spend on homework and studying, as well as the general difficulty of each assignment. Do not take these decisions lightly, but at the same time, do not let them overwhelm you. Choosing classes should be an exciting part of your high school process.

> **A** Seriously. Your <u>classes</u> determine everything. You know how you usually spend time complaining to your friends about that one teacher or about that one super annoying class in which the only work you get is busy work? Try to avoid that situation

altogether, if you can help it. I loved choosing my classes each year (especially electives) because I knew that if I considered my choices carefully, I (probably) would not regret them.

It is true that colleges regard an Honors, IB, or AP level class differently from a regular one. However, there are so many other factors that should determine your decision about each class.

Consider your <u>favorite subjects</u>. With which classes do you want to spend the most time? Students often prefer math and science over social studies and English, or vice versa.

A I'm an "<u>English person</u>," but I wasn't afraid to challenge myself with math classes. However, especially as I've gotten older and have had more freedom to play around with my schedule a bit, I have tried to take more English classes and electives. I was able to take AP English, advanced journalism, and creative writing during my senior year.

Are you a foreign language person? Do you like one subject so much more than the others that you should take electives (and perhaps two academic classes) within that department? Colleges like to see that you challenge yourself in your favorite academic areas. For example, perhaps math is just not your thing, but you are a brilliant writer. Consider taking an Honors or AP English option and staying with regular math. Not only will this choice most likely suit your grades (you will likely achieve higher grades in subjects that are strong for you), but this choice would also suit your time management. Because Honors and AP classes tend to be associated with more work, you will eventually wind up spending more time on your favorite subjects.

What do you see yourself doing with your <u>life</u>?

A I know I'm not the only one overwhelmed by this question. Doesn't it seem as if every adult in the world asks you this as a means of making polite conversation? I actually don't mind that much, as long as people don't expect me to know exactly <u>what my plan is</u>.

Do you find certain careers fascinating? Do you have an adult role model who loves his/her job? Since seventy percent of college students change their majors after they enroll, it is totally okay (and normal) not to know what you want to do when you grow up, but some students do develop an idea in high school. If you might want to be an engineer, for example, you most likely should challenge yourself in higher-level math and science <u>courses</u>.

A For example, one of my friends wants to be a physicist when she grows up, and during senior year, when some of her AP classes conflicted, she dropped AP economics instead of <u>AP BC calculus</u>.

Students interested in engineering or architecture need to plan ahead more than other students because of the specific and time-consuming requirements. If your <u>dream job</u> is an editor, clearly you should try to challenge yourself in English. Taking advanced classes in subject areas that might correspond to your major will also help you when filling out your "intended major" on college applications. While many students do decide to apply to schools without declaring their majors, colleges love to see that you have a passion in certain academic subject areas you intend to pursue.

A Whenever people ask me what I plan to do in terms of a <u>career</u>, I say that I don't know yet, but I do know what I *don't* want to do. For example, I'm almost positive (because nothing is definite) that I have no interest in engineering or participating in the pre-med track. I know that I will want a job in which I can both write and help other people in some capacity, but that's about it at this point. My parents have always told me that college is an incredible time to find a passion; how can anyone expect 17-year-olds applying for college to know what they want to do for the rest of their lives?

Sometimes, the class you choose is based entirely upon the <u>teacher</u>.

A So true. I feel as though my classes with my favorite <u>teachers</u> fly by, whereas the classes with my not-so-favorite teachers take much longer.

Do you love amazing teachers? Clearly, no one prefers a "bad" teacher, but some students care more about their teachers than do others. Are you someone who develops a personal relationship with teachers? Do you like teachers who constantly offer extra help to review material? Schools tend to assign their best teachers to the hardest classes. For some people, a teacher is not a reason to take a class, but if you have ever had the amazing experience of a life-changing teacher, you might think differently.

I know several students who have elected to take particular classes simply because of the <u>teacher</u>.

A This is me. I *love* some of my high school <u>teachers</u>; they made the class experience completely unique and amazing compared to what it would have been with someone else. I always prioritized having good teachers (or teachers I thought I would like as a best guess) over having friends in my classes or even a mutual free period with a friend. I really believe that teachers can change everything. They have the power to make seemingly boring topics beyond interesting, and make you see texts in ways you never thought possible. I honestly don't know where I would be today without some of my favorite teachers; I would go so far as to say that they helped shape the type of person and student I am.

For example, I became really close with my ninth grade Honors English teacher, and I ended up having her for English and journalism throughout my entire high school career. She not only got to know me on an academic level but on a personal level, and by my junior year I asked her for advice on a regular basis. She helped me manage my stress during APs (Advanced Placement) and negotiate my classmates' competitive attitudes during the college application process. I remember one instance when I was freaking out about a test grade in 11AP English—it had a lot of weight in determining my quarter grade and it was much lower than my typical marks. I'll never forget the conversation when she convinced me that getting a "B" in my favorite subject was okay. I am really able to trust her because I've known her for such a long time. It's amazing when you can have teachers for multiple years during high school.

Skilled educators are some of the finest human beings on Earth. If you challenge yourself in class and seek them out for assistance, you never know what can happen. Teachers can open your eyes to possibilities and questions that you never would have considered. They can make you completely engaged in a subject you previously hated. If your school allows you to change your schedule in the beginning of the year, try to balance your teachers with your workload as well. Usually, teachers develop some kind of reputation concerning how much work they assign or how challenging the class is. Make sure that you will be able to handle the work in all your subjects.

Higher-level classes tend to inspire more interesting and stimulating discussions. Are you someone who thrives in a debate setting? Do you enjoy reading assignments? Is there the expectation to do your homework completely and well? While school is school regardless of the classes you take, you would most likely receive a better whole education in an Honors or AP class than you would in a regular class. You might feel more prepared for college-level work in the long run if you challenge yourself in high school. However, there is something to be said for taking a regular class. First of all, having a balance in your life is important. If taking five Honors classes would overwhelm you, consider taking two or three instead. It's equally important to live a balanced life that includes time for family, friends, and your extracurricular activities.

A I'm really glad that I decided to take regular-level science classes throughout most of high school because science is not my thing and Honors classes would have taken up so much extra study time. Also, I was able to achieve higher grades in the easier science classes, which was nice for my GPA since I took so many other Honors and AP classes.

Especially because the academic day typically starts early in the morning at most high schools, you also need to get enough sleep. When you consider all these pieces of your life, it might be difficult to make time for any Honors or AP courses per year. This is okay! Only you (and your family) can decide how much is too much. If you are better off in all regular classes, so be it. Don't beat yourself up about it; just do your best—that should always be good enough. Do not challenge yourself beyond the point at which the workload interferes with your psychological health. I have spoken to many admission counselors at elite colleges and I am confident that students are not judged simply by the number of AP and other advanced credits they earned by the end of senior year.

It is also completely permissible to start high school by taking only a few (or no) higher-level classes and then increasing your workload as you mature. As a mother, I believe in this method. As a college counselor, I have seen success with this plan over and over again. Some students simply require more time than others to figure out studying strategies and time management. Colleges admire students who recognize their ability, and when you take even one more Honors or AP class than you did the year before, you demonstrate growth. Not even the most selective colleges expect to see 12 APs on a transcript.

A What I've seen with my friends who are overachievers is that if you take higher-level classes in every subject starting in ninth grade, there is no possible way to go anywhere but down. This is okay if you'll be able to handle the workload, but maybe consider taking one fewer hard class and adding that subject the next year.

Lastly, consider realistically how you will perform in a higher-level class. Your grades *will* matter, and colleges like to see As and Bs regardless of your class level. It is important to prioritize your grade point average and class rank and make certain that the difficulty of a class will not prevent you from achieving good test grades. Make sure that you can handle the work you sign up for. However, keep in mind that huge state schools often do not have time to read your application line by line. They want to glance at your transcript quickly and see As. Many selective public colleges do admissions by some formula. Often, public schools require higher standards for admission of out-of-state students than for in-state students. I am oversimplifying here, but if you think you will apply mostly to state schools, you may want to consider your projected grade in a class more heavily than the level of class. In contrast, smaller private schools have more time for your individual application, and are more likely to overlook one lower grade if they see that you have challenged yourself with more difficult courses. Many private schools are looking to see evidence that you took a challenging high school curriculum. They will look at your grades for each year in high school and look for any dips or unusual patterns.

Importantly, enroll in the classes you think you will enjoy. High school classes take a lot of your time and commitment, and deserve your attention. Try to savor the opportunity to learn about things that interest you and subjects that will open your eyes and mind to new possibilities.

CHAPTER 3

Choosing High School Extracurricular Activities

It's easy to get caught up in the discussion of which extracurricular activities "look good" for colleges. However, there is no magical formula; with the exception of athletics, a college will not *Reject* or *Accept* you on the basis of any one extracurricular activity. If you are brilliant at something specific like playing the bassoon, that may get you in, but certainly you will be competing with other top bassoonists and a college band only needs one or two. Therefore, what is most important is that you really stay true to yourself throughout high school and participate in the activities that are meaningful and enjoyable for you. Don't get lumped in with your entire class and do something just because your friends are doing it. While it's great to convince your friends to join clubs with you (especially as an overwhelmed freshman), it is more essential to participate in activities to which you can see yourself contributing in a helpful and efficient capacity. Extracurricular "impact" within college admissions is something that has greatly evolved over the last 20 years, and it is an aspect of your application that should not be overlooked and dismissed as unimportant.

A I'd say that the <u>extracurricular</u> portion of my Common App actually took up a large portion of my time spent applying to college. I considered the order of my activities (in terms of importance to me) and did a lot of reflecting to see where I improved a club at any point throughout high school. Extracurricular activities were a huge part of my high school life and I wanted colleges to see that commitment documented in my application.

My first tip is for ninth-graders: sign up for several <u>clubs</u>.

A Mom, I distinctly remember a car ride with you at the end of the summer before ninth grade. You (very warmly) explained to me the importance of high school grades and <u>activities</u>. Although I knew you were trying to help me, I felt overwhelmed and annoyed. Of course, I was going to try a million activities after attending the club fair! However, I am so glad that we have always discussed the importance of my high school decisions. The truth is, they do matter, and you don't want to have any regrets when it comes time to apply for college.

Your interests and abilities will evolve over time, and you don't know where one club meeting will lead you in the future. While a faculty advisor and older students in the clubs can be factors when considering which organizations to sign up for at first, if you like the idea of a <u>club</u>, just join.

A I may have gone a little nuts at the <u>club</u> fair in ninth grade; I must have signed up for at least 15 clubs. While it was hard to decline some clubs' invitations to meetings because I simply did not have time for everything, I developed preferences for a handful of clubs pretty naturally. I stuck with my favorites throughout high school and they have really shaped my interests. Because I've been involved with each club for such a long time, I have developed personal relationships with a few advisors. It is so nice to have a few adults in school who can advocate and care for you.

I'm all about making commitments and sticking to them, but in ninth grade I think you get a "free pass" with clubs. Because most freshmen begin high school in a new building, it is expected and encouraged that students will be open to various clubs all year, especially within the first few months. As freshman year progresses, try to identify a few clubs that really intrigue you. Which club meetings ignited a passion in you? Which clubs are the ones to which you will want to dedicate the most time? There is no "right" number of how many clubs you should join; commit to as many as your time allows.

> **A** If I had had more time, I would have participated in more clubs. However, it is simply not possible to dedicate a real commitment to 15 clubs. Make sure you stick with the ones you actually care about.

It is certainly nice if you can land a titled leadership position such as *president* or *secretary* when you get older in high school, but it is far more important to make a significant contribution to the club. Titles do not actually mean that much; it's more than fine if you are a "quiet leader." My suggestion is that you find a niche in a few clubs and make a real, visible difference. When Amanda was ending her sophomore year, her debate team faced threats of completely dissolving because of some rules broken by the upperclassmen. Although Amanda did not hold a leadership position at the time, she, along with two of her friends, committed herself to rebuilding and reviving the dying team. The group met with a council of teachers, potential new advisors, and the high school principal. Eventually, with the help of the administration, the debate team was not only reinstated for Amanda's junior year at Great Neck South, but was also thriving by the end of that term. This is an example of Amanda making a difference in the club without being a "president," and it was something she wrote about on college applications when asked how she had contributed to the debate team. It is fine to hold a position, but what you *do* with that position is what counts; Amanda's contribution as an untitled member meant more to the club than anything done by the senior who was the "president" in name only.

Extracurricular activities are all about balancing and managing your time between your schoolwork and your passions (hence *extra*curricular). After freshman year, when you have a sense of your typical workload, you should commit to only activities that you will be able to do well. There's no sense in being a part of a dozen clubs and barely going to any meetings because they conflict with one another. Instead, choose the handful that mean the most to you—the ones in which you hope to lead during your junior and senior years. Colleges are negatively sensitive to very long activity lists and sometimes see these résumés as embellished. Commitment is dedicating significant time to each club. Amanda worked on her high school newspaper for the entirety of her Great Neck South career, and it was typical for students to apply for top leadership positions just before their senior year. Although Amanda was a strong contender for the Editor-in-Chief position, she elected to submit an application for a second highest position, Print Managing Editor. It was important to her to perform well in all her activities, and she did not feel as if she had the time to commit to the Editor-in-Chief responsibilities. A common misconception is that you should always take the highest leadership honor available to you, but this is not always the wisest decision. Think carefully about how much time you will have to dedicate to something in order to do it to the best of your ability.

It was actually tough to let go of the "Editor-in-Chief" position for my senior year. However, it all comes back again to impact. I feel as if I made the most of my Print Managing Editor position by tailoring the position to my specific leadership abilities and goals for the year. I was also innovative in bringing new ideas to the club that I would not have had the time for had I been the Editor-in-Chief.

In terms of <u>community service</u>, there are plenty of opportunities within your own neighborhood if you seek them out.

A Within my school alone there is a handful of <u>service-oriented clubs and activities</u>. Joining at least one will ensure that you have community service on your résumé. But don't just do it for the résumé, do it for the good. Helping other people makes you feel good about yourself. For example, one of my favorite ways to help out in my community is to go to a senior citizens' living center. Just talking to the residents and participating in events such as bingo and card games brings them so much joy.

Be a diligent participant and develop genuine relationships with the people you want to help. You do *not* need to travel across the globe to do service. In fact, many colleges frown upon travel-service trips because they see this as a "rich kid" benefit; they view those students as people who wanted to go somewhere extraordinary and "look good" for college simultaneously. However, there are exceptions to my rule: I once had a student who was dedicated to both marine biology and photography—an interesting combination. His family had the financial resources to send him all over the world (like Fiji) to explore his interests, and he came home with truly phenomenal photos of fish and wildlife under the sea, and hours of community service.

Several years ago, it used to be that if students were "well-rounded" in high school, they were "good to go" for college admissions. Now, more of the top colleges look for a well-rounded *class*, not necessarily <u>well-rounded</u> individual students.

A I found this hard to believe. Especially as someone who does not necessarily have one "hook" (a specific attribute that might separate you from other college applicants), I had to stay focused on <u>many activities</u> throughout high school.

However, many liberal arts schools still want well-rounded people. As a mom and an educator, I just tell my students to stay true to themselves. Of course, you should be active in your school and community, but be authentically involved. Don't try to game the system or do something because you think it will "look good."

I make one of my favorite jokes when clients ask me whether their activities will be "good enough" to get them into Harvard. I say that unless he/she has cured cancer, it is doubtful. An article from January 2016 in *The Washington Post* titled "To get into college, Harvard report advocates for kindness instead of overachieving," explains Harvard's supposed new stance that students should focus on kindness over achievement. Could this be real? This would mean that my middle-income, kind, hardworking, "straight A" students who mindfully participate in meaningful activities have a chance at any college. But even if this is not true, let's also remember that there are thousands of college options in our country. And, I would argue that hundreds of them offer a better, more intentional education than some of the schools at the top. (Look for more on this topic in Chapter 28 on *Mulling the Future*.)

It is equally important to get over being the president of everything. The word *president* is often overrated in the college admissions process. There are literally thousands of *presidents* applying to college from all over the country; from just one school with 20 clubs alone, that's likely 20 presidents, 20 vice presidents, 20 secretaries...you get the point. Being president is just not special enough—it's your contribution to the club that counts.

One of my friends was ecstatic when she was elected the president of a club for her senior year. However, I'm not so sure she wanted that position for the right reasons. As senior year progressed and she got *Accepted* to more and more colleges, it became evident that she had wanted this position only for the title; she stopped coming to meetings and positively contributing to the club. Don't be the person who only joins a club to pad a

...ing, stick around for more of your senior year ...u'll get to enjoy all the fun aspects of your clubs ...us much pressure from your classes.

If you are an athlete who intends to continue a sport in college, the application process can be totally different. Many strong athletes are so busy playing one sport in high school that they do not have time for other extracurriculars. If you love one sport, it is good that you are spending time enjoying it. However, you are undoubtedly missing a great deal of what should be a well-rounded high school experience. Sometimes, pressure for athletes can be overwhelming because students feel the need to help financially by getting a college athletic scholarship. With tuition costs on the rise, I get it. However, athletic deals initially promised by coaches will fall through sometimes. You never know if you will injure yourself in a way that prevents you from playing again. It is important to keep your college options open and to try your best academically, regardless of your athletic talent. By keeping your grades up, you are less likely to get burned. It's also nice if you can find the time for at least one club. If you decide for some reason that you do not want to play sports in college, at least you will have explored other interests in high school.

CHAPTER 4

Preparing During the Summer

While many people may disagree with me, I firmly believe that summers are supposed to be fun. I do not think it is necessary to take any extra classes or study for the ACT or SAT for the better part of each summer. Summer is a special time when you can let loose and enjoy yourself so that you are reenergized for each school year.

No, you should not sleep the summer away or watch television for five hours a day. However, there are other ways to relax and have fun but also <u>occupy your time</u> by contributing in a meaningful way to your community.

> **A** I can't imagine sitting around and doing nothing for weeks on end. As tempting as it may seem in June, you'll get tired of it. A few of my friends were at first very excited about their decision to literally make no plans for one summer. However, they said it was the most boring summer ever. I think it can be fun to have maybe <u>one or two weeks of unstructured time</u> if that sounds enticing, but longer than that will likely get dull.

If you have a passion, pursue it over the summer. Have you always wanted to learn to play an instrument? Go to a day camp for a particular sport? Participate in research? Learn about television production? Take culinary classes?

> **A** You'd be surprised (at least I was) at the number of classes your local adult or teen community center offers. If you live near a city, look into opportunities there as well. There are so many things to do.

Do what interests you most because if you enjoy yourself, your summers can radiate in your application and give the admission readers a sense of who you are outside school. Regardless of the activity, make sure you have a schedule that includes something besides sitting on your couch. Colleges want to see that you will contribute to their communities, and what better way to demonstrate that than to voluntarily participate in a local program? Plus, your mind will stay sharper if you focus on something other than a screen for the summer. Also plan to read regularly—it can be a book you enjoy.

If you are looking to make some extra money during the summer, working in a local ice cream shop—although potentially dangerous for the waistline—is as good as any job. Don't underestimate the fact that you will have to show responsibility, dedication, and diligence to commit to any simple job. These qualities can all bloom on your application and be advantageous to you for any future endeavor. Also, it is great to show on your application that you have the ability to keep a job for an extended period of time; it shows you work well with others and can take directions from a boss. There are plenty of job opportunities during the summer if you seek them out. Whether you want to scoop ice cream, walk people to tables as a restaurant host/hostess, play with little kids in summer day care, or even file records at a clerical desk job, many local businesses look to hire responsible high school students over the summer. The important thing is to plan ahead and not wait until April to begin thinking about where you might want to work.

If you think you might want to pursue a particular career path but you don't have much experience (and you have the luxury of not having to work over the summer), see if you can get an internship. Sometimes internships are paid and sometimes they are not, but regardless, the experience can be fantastic and could help you navigate your college major a little more smoothly. Internships can even ignite a new interest and make you consider unexpected pursuits. I have had many students come away from internships that really helped shape their hopes and plans for college. Many students, especially those interested in science, love doing research in a lab as an intern, which can also prove to be a very valuable experience. Because high schools often link their science departments to these types of programs, see what you can secure for yourself during the school year by achieving well in science classes.

Even after what I have said about enjoying yourself during the summer, always <u>consider your interests</u>. If your high school does not offer Italian but you have always wanted to study it, go learn it! Taking classes during the summer because of genuine interest can be a terrific way to demonstrate your intellectual and academic curiosity. Even if you won't get high school credit for a class, it may still be worth your time if you will really enjoy the subject matter.

A If I were ever home during the summer, I would definitely take advantage of time for classes that don't fit into my schedule in high school. For example, <u>I have always wanted to study American Sign Language</u>, and I hope to do so in college or at some point in the future.

Volunteer work, paid work, research, local community service, and internships are all great ways to spend a summer. If you can be innovative and link your interests with pursuing career goals, that will demonstrate your commitment, dedication, and thoughtfulness in planning a summer. I have worked with several athletes who not only love playing their sport, but also love teaching it, so they either volunteered or sought a paid position giving lessons to younger children. Another student ran soccer birthday parties— combining his interests in soccer and working with <u>children</u>.

> **A** During a school vacation one year, I combined my interests of acting and singing and working with <u>kids</u> when I helped direct my synagogue's annual holiday/Chanukah show. The kids were so cute and I had a really good time. Although I was not paid, this was an important experience for me in developing leadership skills.

Amanda spent her high school summers at her sleep-away camp and progressed from a camper to a counselor-in-training (CIT) to a full-time <u>counselor</u>.

> **A** I honestly can't imagine a summer without camp. I'm happy that I did not have to stop going there and was able to bridge my camper and <u>counselor</u> years with my experience as a CIT. A camp experience I had during my first summer as a counselor ended up providing inspiration for my Common App essay (see Chapter 27 for my sample essay).

Regardless of what you choose to do, my recommendation is to make summers as much fun as possible for yourself! Enjoy the weather and allow your brain to take a break.

CHAPTER 5

Understanding Standardized Testing

Standardized testing receives a lot of emphasis from most high schools and many universities, and it is true that it is an important aspect of your application. When spending so much money and countless hours on test preparation, remember that usually (because the tests are standardized) a student's score will only go up so much. Some students literally spend years practicing with tutors and attending classes that do not necessarily yield better results. While I have seen students go from an average score to one well above average, they are the exceptions, not the norm. Don't expect more from yourself than what you can realistically achieve.

SATs and ACTs are considered equal tests by college admissions counselors throughout the country; it's a myth that one is preferred over the other. At the time of writing this, the new SAT is still in its early stages. It is yet to be determined how this will change the landscape of standardized testing, so I have been recommending that most students take the ACT for now until we are able to analyze how the new SAT concordance chart works.

Personally, I've been a fan of the ACT over the SAT for years. I maintain that the ACT test is more representative of high school curricula, as opposed to results based upon tips or tricks that students often study prior to sitting for the SAT tests. However, the College Board changed the SAT in a big way in 2016 to make it more similar to the current ACT.

> I'm the only one among my friends who did not even attempt the SAT for real. I quickly discovered that the ACT was more my speed for a test, even though the timing took some adjustment. I generally preferred to knock out each subject in one time block, instead of switching back and forth between math and English like the old SAT layout. And, believe it or not, my mom did not make me take the ACT. While she certainly expressed her preference for the ACT over the SAT, of course she wanted me to take the test with which I felt more comfortable.

This leads to the big, personal question for each high school student: SAT or ACT? A major difference between the two testing companies is in philosophy: The College Board (SAT company) owns your tests. While you can opt for "score choice" and select which colleges see which tests (paying extra money to do so), in rare cases this can end up backfiring because some colleges are clearly stating on their websites that they do not want their applicants to use score choice. Essentially, if a score is part of your College Board testing history, the college wants to see your score.

> This sounds super scary to me. Truthfully, I was really nervous when I first started to take standardized tests, and it took time for me to adjust to my testing ritual. After my first few tests, I learned what I could say to myself to feel motivated and pumped up.

Unless you pay more for score choice, the College Board will send *all* of your scores to requested colleges—including your subject tests, also known as "SAT IIs." The ACT, however, believes that *you* own your test scores and have the right to cancel them at any time.

> Once you delete an ACT test, there isn't any way possible to see your score again on your account; it's gone forever.

Each test is regarded as a separate entity, not a part of your testing history. But if a college does not participate in score choice, this doesn't help you.

Ever since I began my career as a school counselor, I have recommended to my students that under mock testing conditions (no cell phone or interruptions), they should tackle one practice SAT and one practice ACT in order to see which test results in a higher score and which one was preferable to take.

> **A** I totally think everyone should do this. Over spring break of my sophomore year, I took a practice ACT on a Saturday and a practice SAT on the very next day. Although it was an exhausting weekend, I wanted to get the diagnostics out of the way. And especially because I knew I'd be away for the entire summer at camp, I wanted to have a game plan for the beginning of junior year.

Many students feel the need to take both tests for real, but that is neither necessary nor necessarily beneficial.

> **A** I tried not to look at people as if they were crazy when they told me that they were preparing for both the SAT and the ACT. But...why? Why would anyone want to do that? To me, it makes so much more sense to take practice tests that don't count and then immediately determine which test you like better. Afterwards, just focus on taking that one test until you reach your target score. What's even worse is not realizing that the *other* test is better for you until you've wasted so much time and money on the first. For example, my friend was positive that he would like the SAT better, and had a tutor for five months before he took his first test— and bombed it. I felt terrible when he discovered that he could ace the ACT with barely any preparation at all. What a waste of a tutor and precious junior year time!

Especially considering that the College Board might submit all your scores to colleges regardless of whether you did well or not, it may not be the best idea to take an SAT unless you have really prepared for it. That said, recent news reports show that increasing numbers of students are submitting both the SAT and ACT to top colleges that when asked say that they prefer having all that information. I still maintain that it is good to prepare for one test and stick with it, but similar to many aspects of college admissions, I will keep an eye on how trends develop, especially with the new SAT. Before registering for both tests (especially in the next couple of years), consider that you will likely be a "guinea pig" for the new SAT. This could eventually work to your advantage, but know what you are signing up for. While it is fine to try both tests for real, I honestly think that this is a waste of time and money; focus on one test and really get good at it.

Remember to keep in mind that standardized testing is only one factor in college admissions; it is not the "be all, end all" determinant. Certainly, some colleges and majors rely on your results more than others. A NACAC (National Association for College Admission Counseling) survey that collected data from more than 400 college campuses across the country reported that although a majority of institutions require students to submit SAT or ACT scores, only half of these schools actually track how well standardized testing predicts success in college. However, now there are more than 950 colleges that offer flexible testing options. You don't even *have to* take the tests if you don't want to. I highly recommend that you look at some of these schools to take the pressure off your standardized testing: fairtest.org.

> **A** Before we were confident in my ability to reach a relatively high score on the ACT, I found great security in knowing I could apply to some pretty decent schools without even submitting standardized tests. Look into them during your freshman and sophomore years so that you won't worry as much (and therefore perform better) when you attempt the tests later in high school.

Athletes and students applying for scholarships especially need to double-check policies. Sometimes colleges that are test-optional require testing for athletes (per NCAA requests) and/or for merit-based scholarship contenders, and may want to see scores before awarding scholarship money. When colleges only "recommend" testing, that is another varied nuance. Your best bet is to clarify policies with each specific college if you are unsure about submitting your scores.

As a side note, I always recommend that you try the essay for either test, even if most schools on your list do not consider it. This is for a few reasons. First, when you make the decision not to take the essay, your college list will likely not be finalized. Second, if your grades improve down the road, you may add different competitive colleges to your list and find that you have to retake a test because you did not take the essay section previously.

You might also consider submitting SAT IIs, also known as *Subject Tests*, with your application (formerly known as *Achievement Tests*). Essentially, these are hour-long exams on specific subjects. For example, the College Board offers SAT IIs in a few sciences, languages, math levels, English, and history topics. Here are some frequently asked questions and answers that I get from students concerning subject tests:

Do I Need to Take SAT IIs?

It will depend on where you apply, but probably not. While they can be beneficial to any application if you do well, fewer than 30 colleges in the country actually require Subject Tests. Many colleges "recommend" the tests and prefer to see them, but by no means should you think that you don't have a good chance anywhere if you choose not to submit these tests. The Ivies and top-tiers sometimes want them, but like so many factors, it can depend on your major and interests. If you will be applying to ultra-selective schools, having several Subject Tests in the 700s is a good idea. When colleges "recommend" them, they usually expect you to take them.

Should I Take SAT IIs in Ninth Grade?

This is really not necessary; give yourself ample time in your first year of high school to study for your finals and keep your grade point average as high as possible.

> **A** Almost all of my friends took the biology SAT II when we were freshmen, even those students who were in Regents biology. However, I knew that I would be competing against students in AP and Honors bio, so my mom (smartly) recommended that I not take that test.

At the beginning of your second semester in sophomore year and junior year, decide which tests make the most sense for you to take. Which APs are you taking? Which tests are the ones for which you would like to spend time preparing?

> **A** Just a quick side story that shows the importance of diligence when registering for any test: one of my friends was supposed to take an SAT II in June of ninth grade. When she arrived at the testing center, the proctors informed her that she was actually signed up for the SAT I! Just make sure that you are double- and triple-checking your registration details before you submit forms.

What Is a "Good" Score?

Scoring a 700 or higher on any subject test shows clear mastery of the material. Because only a few dozen colleges actually require Subject Tests, I do not recommend that my students send scores below 700. Only highly competitive, top-tier schools require SAT IIs and typically receive many highly qualified students' applications. If you are scoring in the 400s or 500s on practice tests, it is probably not a good use of your time to prepare for that Subject Test.

A I decided to take a practice literature SAT II to see how I would score, and I did terribly. Because there essentially is no content to review for that test, I decided not to waste my time.

Don't waste your money. However, if you are scoring in the 600s on practice, do whatever you can to give yourself a little boost to the 700 mark (even in the ninth grade). If you are a strong test taker, you might as well play to your strengths and take several subject tests—why not? Strong scores will only help your application.

As a general rule of thumb, colleges tend to prefer testing from your junior and senior years in high school and weigh your performance on these exams more heavily.

A This may have been a mistake on my part, but I actually took only one SAT II before my junior year: the math level one. And because I did not do well, I had no respectable scores going into junior year. That was a very stressful feeling. If you think you're going to apply to some top-tier colleges, try to at least have one good score under your belt before the craziness of junior year.

Not only are the tests more recent, but they are also likely a more accurate reflection of how you will perform academically in your first year in college.

Students should make a testing plan and strategy based on their personal circumstances. For example, a dedicated soccer player may not want to plan for a standardized test prep push in the fall because he/she realizes that that will be an extremely busy season. Typically (although there are plenty of exceptions), I work with families who are anxious to get started with standardized testing. To calm their nerves, I usually recommend that these students take a practice/diagnostic SAT and ACT by the end of tenth grade. In some states and schools, this is a requirement. However, I do not believe that there is a one-size-fits-all-approach to testing, and students should prepare at a pace that suits their individual needs and learning styles. Consulting with your school counselor can help you determine what makes the most sense for you.

A I have always been one to get work done as soon as possible. I started preparing for my ACT in August before my junior year and hoped to be finished by February. Unfortunately, I wasn't quite satisfied with my score until September of the following year. I kept taking the test because I didn't want to have any regrets when it came time to apply to college.

If you are enrolled in AP classes, you should take the exam at the end of each class. Taking more APs is not necessarily better, but if you are lucky enough to attend a high school that offers several different AP options, you should absolutely take advantage of them (if that's appropriate for your level in the subject). Advanced Placement classes culminating in the exams are opportunities to save some money earmarked for college if you score high enough on the test (although score requirements vary for each college, major, and program). I do not think it is necessary to take too many APs. There is no magic number, but, typically, I find that academically strong students who take eight to ten APs throughout high school are pushing themselves while still finding time for a balance of other activities in their lives.

A Yep—I agree with that. I took one sophomore year, three junior year, and four senior year (totaling eight). While high school has definitely been academically challenging for me (especially during junior year with the added pressure of standardized testing), I have been able to dedicate adequate time to my extracurriculars, family, friends, and sleep.

I have informally interviewed admission counselors at some Ivy League schools and I have been told repeatedly that while students should challenge themselves, a crazy number of APs is not necessary or even suggested. As a mom and an educator, I would argue that finding a balance is important here, and colleges seem to agree. They want their prospective students doing more interesting things with their time than studying for a test.

If you possess the right <u>mindset</u>, the standardized testing part of high school does not have to consume your life. Although it's a lot, you can balance your preparation with other, meaningful activities and commitments.

> **A** My biggest piece of advice for standardized testing is to develop a <u>mantra</u> and testing ritual that you perform before the big day. I found that my confidence grew tremendously when I would tell myself, "Amanda, you got this. You're ready," before a test. I said it over and over. Don't doubt yourself because you'll never do well with a negative attitude (more in Chapter 23 on *Keeping the Proper Perspective*).

While you should probably do some outside research on both standardized exams to see which test better suits your style, there is a quick comparison between the ACT and SAT (new as of March 2016). See the table on pages 36–37.

Please note that Amanda's comments follow the chart, as indicated with numbers.

SAT (new as of March 2016)	**ACT**
General	
Two section scores: reading/ writing & math	Four section scores: English, math, reading, science
Scoring: 400–1600 total	Scoring: 1–36 composite[1]
Four sections	Four sections
Math	
58 math questions; avg. time 83s/question	60 math questions; avg. time 60s/question[2]
One no-calculator section; one calculator section	Allowed to use a calculator on all questions, although most can be solved without one[3]
Range of math: advanced algebra, interpretation of data, geometry and arithmetic, trigonometry	Range of math: geometry, algebra, arithmetic, trigonometry
Reading	
52 questions; avg. time 75s/question	40 questions; avg. time 53s/question[4]
17% of questions test vocabulary	8% of questions test vocabulary
Four long passages; two medium passages	Four long passages; one is usually a comparison
Types of passages: 1 prose, 1 social science/history, 2 sciences, 1 global discussion	Types of passages: 1 prose, 1 social science, 1 humanities (usually comparison), 1 natural sci.
English/Writing	
44 questions; avg. time 48s/question	75 questions; avg. time 36s/question[5]
7% of questions test vocabulary	3% of questions test vocabulary
Grammar tested: punctuation, words in context, sentence structure	Grammar tested: punctuation, sentence structure

SAT	ACT
Essay	
Not mandatory; 50 minutes	Not mandatory; 40 minutes
Three section scores: reading, analysis, writing	Four section scores: ideas/analysis, development/support, organization, language use/convention
Cannot use personal opinion	Use personal opinion while addressing all three viewpoints
Prompt: a short passage that students must analyze	Prompt: a contemporary issue with three different opinions to consider

1. Personally, I like this scale a lot more than the SAT; it's so much easier to know where you stand compared to other students.

2. I'm not going to lie: this can be rough, especially on the harder questions toward the end. Because the ACT math test progresses (approximately) from the easiest to the hardest questions, try to zip through the first 20 or 30 in under a minute per question so you can bank more time for the end.

3. Don't use your calculator unless you need it because you don't have time to spare.

4. I also always found this section a definite time crunch. When you read, make sure you're totally in the zone to focus. Also, don't flip out if you can't find the answer to a question; just skip it and move on. During my first ever real ACT, I panicked midway through the reading section and didn't get to finish trying the questions even though I had done fine with timing in practice.

5. This sounds really quick, but I (and many of my friends) actually found this to be the easiest section. I usually finished comfortably with 10 minutes to spare and check over my work. While section preferences depend on the person, I wouldn't recommend rushing on English. There is really so much time to get everything done.

PART II

LOGISTICS OF APPLYING TO COLLEGE

CHAPTER 6

Staying Proactive and Starting Early

The advice from my perspective is pretty simple: stay on top of your work so that you are not overwhelmed at the end. While you certainly do not have to start the college process too early, there are definitely things you can do to make the process more efficient when you are ready to begin.

It is important to meet with your <u>high school counselor regularly</u>—even if it's not required by your high school.

> **A** In my high school, freshmen and sophomores have to meet with their counselors only once, and juniors only twice. While initially I was very against arranging meetings with my school counselor, essentially for nothing important—just to talk to her—this was one of my mom's better pieces of advice. The truth is, you'll want your letters of recommendation to be strong, and how can your counselor write good, descriptive letters if he/she has met you only four times for 20-minute periods? And what I discovered by meeting with my school counselor more often during my junior and senior years is that I really liked her. Your school counselor is someone who will keep all academic information confidential, and someone who can answer all your questions (even the tiny, annoying ones) about your college applications. When I submitted most of my applications, <u>I talked to my high school counselor almost daily.</u> Each night I would discover that I had more questions, and I would

walk into the office during my free period to ask them. Trust me, you will have a lot of questions. Even *I* had a lot of questions, and I had probably the most helpful mom of anyone in my grade. For example, something such as your exact class size or the terminology your school uses to refer to Honors pre-calculus, are bits of information that really only your school counselor can supply.

Typically, school counselors are nice, caring people who are overworked with large caseloads. When I was a school counselor, my caseload topped out at 300 students; however, in some public high schools around the country, counselors are responsible for close to 1,000 students. If your school counselor is too busy or unresponsive, seek help elsewhere from a trusted resource.

Although your school counselor is probably in charge of so many people, he/she will be writing your counselor letter of recommendation (more in Chapter 13 on *Getting Letters of Recommendation*) and won't have anything to say if you do not make an effort to visit the guidance office. If you can make a minimum of two guidance appointments per year, you are on a good track. It almost doesn't matter what you talk about: scheduling, teachers for next year, a certain college, major, whatever you want.

Realistically, you could have several legitimate questions for your school counselor without thinking too hard about it. For example, ask him/her about a certain high school course offered for seniors only. Ask how you can get a summer internship. Regardless of what you ask, your visit to the guidance office shows initiative, something your school counselor can mention in his/her letter of recommendation.

The intention here is for you to help your school counselor connect your name to your face and personality, and get to know who you are. When it comes time for the counselor to write your letter of recommendation, you will want to be more than simply a name on a long, alphabetized list, something accomplished only by getting to know each other.

Time management is not really something you can learn, but is rather a strategy for productivity you should develop over time. If you know you tend to push assignments to the last minute, try to plan ahead and know how many schools you will be applying to. Even if you only apply to a handful of colleges, you could end up writing many essays; therefore, it is important to leave yourself enough time for several drafts. Here's a promise, though: your Common App essay and supplements will take longer than you initially think. <u>Not only do you need to brainstorm ideas and generate material</u>, but you also need to edit everything for it to be well written!

A This actually gets pretty exhausting after a while; <u>there is so much to do.</u> There is so much to write; at the beginning, your "to-do" list will seem endless. I remember feeling super overwhelmed once I made a list of all the supplements my schools required. Don't worry, you'll get through it. The work is only temporary.

The activity portion of your application will take a while to compose as well; do not underestimate the importance of dedicating time to this part. You will want to <u>fully utilize the 150-character limit</u> for each activity on the Common App, but this is difficult to accomplish while still getting across your descriptions in a way that the reader can easily understand. I have seen many students scrap several drafts of their Common App activities section before they meet with my approval.

A This was *so difficult*. I felt restricted by the character limit; there was so much to say about each activity. <u>You definitely have to be creative</u> when describing your commitment to your extracurriculars on the Common App. Also, if you submit an extra résumé, you can add flourishes to your responses and descriptions. For example, highlight the importance of a simple activity like babysitting by explaining how you prepared meals, provided comfort to young kids, and initiated new games.

While Common App is designed to make applying to college easier and make the process more standardized and universal for each school, not all colleges use Common App. Most state schools, as well as a few private colleges, have their own applications and do not have the Common App option. If you are using multiple applications, plan to spend a while on the identifying information in each application. For example, you will need to fill out your name, address, phone number, Social Security number, parents' levels of education, and much more.

> **A** And don't mess up! Mom, it was probably not necessary to check and recheck every application's information five or six times. We sure caught every mistake, though.

The state school applications often require a lot of information by hand, and will not always correlate with one another; each college is entitled to its own system of requesting your information. Rather than copying and pasting your activities from the Common App, for example, you often need to rewrite them to fit the character count for each different state school.

> **A** Even though you'll have to adjust the wording for each school, I found it helpful to keep a Word document running of standard phrases and adjectives that I used to describe each activity. Then you can mix-and-match and play around with what you've written in order to synthesize a coherent and succinct response on each application.

One of the intentions of the Coalition for Access is to allow students to start building their applications as early as ninth grade to avoid stress later in high school. The Coalition is a fairly new organizational tool for college-bound high school students, which intends to help students organize their accomplishments for college review. Students can add things such as papers, videos, and clippings to their "lockers" for easy review, compilation, and submission for senior year. (There is more information about this application in Chapter 14 on *Using Common Application, Naviance, Universal Application, Coalition for Access, and More.*)

> **A** Although I can't really comment from personal experience because the Coalition was not an option for my year when applying to college, this sounds kind of interesting if you utilize it well. The most important thing is to keep yourself organized throughout high school; keep track of everything you do, how many hours you spend on each activity, and all correspondence you have with colleges.

Common App usually announces the following year's essay questions in March. While the focus of second-semester junior year should definitely be on keeping up your grade point average and doing well on standardized testing, if you have some extra time, it can be really beneficial for you to consider the Common App essay questions earlier rather than later. You never know if something that happens to you in grade 11 could turn into a brilliant essay.

> **A** Initially, I had a goal of writing my Common App essay during junior year. However, I quickly found that I wanted to spend my spare time reviewing for classroom tests and the ACT instead of on college (understandably). I would suggest having a notebook with you at all times, though. If an idea hits you for an essay, run with it.

Writing your essays and supplements, and even physically filling out applications, can be accomplished during the summer before you even begin senior year. Common App usually goes "live" on August 1, so you cannot complete aspects of the Common App before this date without having the system erase some of your information. However, try to get to it as soon as possible in August. You have the opportunity to make a huge jumpstart before you are potentially drowning in your senior-year workload. Especially if you plan on taking a challenging curriculum during twelfth grade and continuing your extracurricular activities, your college applications are an enormous time-sapper that you are not accustomed to fitting into your schedule. Try to at least have some college work done before classes begin. At the very least, perfect your personal essay over the summer.

A I know that I hardly speak for everyone because I absolutely hate procrastinating. I had 90% of my applications and supplements done before senior year started. I got back from camp on August 14, and I pretty much sat at the kitchen table for two weeks to produce essay after essay after yet another essay. It became a family joke that I was a "machine." I know, this sounds horrible. This was a rough way to end a summer, but I wouldn't have done it any other way. I was so unbelievably happy to be finished writing as most people complained about starting only their first essays after school started. I really got to take advantage of senior year as soon as it began because the bulk of my college work was done. Although there were still things I had to do (plenty, actually) in September and October, I was able to successfully manage my challenging classes and extracurricular activities.

CHAPTER 7

Organizing Everything

Your experience of applying to college will depend a great deal on how well you can keep your materials organized. You won't quite realize how much material you have accumulated through high school until you sit down and sift through what you want to show colleges. One of the Coalition's goals is to make this process easier for students; however, there are other mechanisms you can use to organize yourself. You want to highlight the best of four years of hard work for colleges to evaluate. This is a long process, but <u>organization, I promise, will only make it easier</u>. For Microsoft users, OneNote works well.

> **A** Something I did was <u>make a separate desktop folder</u> for college application-related Word documents, pdfs, and payment receipts. There were several times when I had to refer to work I had already done in order to fill out an application.

<u>Make lists and checklists</u> to keep track of everything you have done and everything you have left to do.

> **A** I may be biased because I am totally a list-maker. However, I truly believe that they are helpful not only in showing you how much you have left to do, but also in giving you an incredible

sense of accomplishment each time you cross off an item. There's nothing more satisfying than checking off that last bullet on your list. Especially because I wrote so many essays in the span of two weeks, I kept a record of every essay I had to write for each college on my list.

Set both short-term and long-term goals. Here is a sample checklist that I have my students complete; feel free to edit it to fit your specific needs. Using an Excel spreadsheet is helpful. Websites are the best place to find up-to-date answers, but because the logistics are fluid and can change regularly, you may have to recheck them occasionally. I remember that Amanda made a quick list of all colleges' testing sites. A one-page spread with just the links helped as an addition to the grid below. Sometimes there is more information than a grid can hold, and having quick link reference can help you easily refer to it multiple times.

	College	College	College	College	College
EA/ED/RD					
LOR					
Testing					
Dem. Interest					
Supplements					
Visits					
Interviews					
Résumé					
Scholarship					
Portfolio					
Type of App					
R&B					
Stud. Faculty					
Honors Pr.					
Grad. Rate					

If you need help getting started or knowing exactly *what* you need to organize throughout the months when applying to college, refer to the following bullet points:

▶ <u>Name of each school</u> (different lists for those to which you are definitely applying and those you might be applying to)

 To simplify the search for a particular school, I found it helpful to <u>alphabetize the list</u> based on the college's name.

▶ Admission rate of Acceptance during the Early and Regular Decision rounds

▶ How level of Demonstrated Interest is evaluated/prioritized (learned through college's institutional research or admissions counselors directly)

▶ Early Decision 1, 2, Regular Decision dates/deadlines to <u>submit applications</u>

 <u>Attack your Early Action and Rolling schools first.</u> (See Chapter 17 on *Assessing Types of Applications and Responses*)

▶ <u>Dates</u> of your previous visits to campus

 On Common App, sometimes the school literally asks for the day and date that you visited, so <u>keep this information for your records.</u> If you have an email folder for each school (I strongly suggest this), you can just save the campus tour/information session confirmation and refer back to it.

▶ Type of application each school accepts (for example: Common App, Coalition for Access, Universal Application, Cappex, or an institution application, which is popular among some state systems such as Apply Texas and the University of California schools)

- Testing requirements and recommendations (ACT, SAT, SAT II, AP scores/credits, test-optional/flexible)
- How to send test scores
- Interview policy and deadline to register. On college websites, check availability of alumni for interviews and admission officers when they visit your local city

> **A** Get on this one as soon as possible! The interview slots book up quickly.

- Supplemental essay prompts
- Any special program or honors program that might interest you (may have different application requirements)

> **A** From my experience these questions usually take the longest, so don't save this work for the end.

- Your password for each college's application (also keep checking your email after you submit to a college). You can also use LastPass, which is a free storage space that stores encrypted passwords

> **A** I'm guilty of not being the best at this in terms of organization. I usually relied on my computer to save my passwords in Keychain. However, this made it so that I could not check any college account from another computer. If you simply keep a handwritten list of all your passwords, you won't ever get stuck.
>
> Sometimes after a college receives your application, it will give you an ID code to use when checking the status of your admissions decision. These codes are often random combinations of numbers and letters, so definitely write them down.

▶ Letters of recommendation (requirements and deadlines; how you should submit them)

> **A** Some colleges have specific guidelines and rules about people who can and cannot write your letters of recommendation, so make sure you double-check before requesting letters. Also, check if colleges want your high school to send the letters by USPS or directly through Naviance or some other electronic system.

▶ Portfolio (if applicable)
▶ High school résumé (if applicable). This would allow you to expand upon activity descriptions beyond the character constraints of most applications. Résumé formats can vary, but they are preferably one to two pages that highlight your participation in school, work experience and summer commitments. ZeeMee (adopted by about 200 colleges nationwide) offers students an opportunity to video personal data and accomplishments to accompany the Common Application. The Coalition offers its own portfolio-style application via an online locker (more details on the Locker in Chapter 14 on *Using Common Application, Naviance, Universal Application, Coalition for Access and More*).

> **A** Not all schools accept them, but some allow you to submit an extracurricular résumé via Common App to elaborate on your commitments. Make use of this opportunity!

CHAPTER 8

Demonstrating Interest and "Playing the Game"

"Demonstrating Interest" in colleges is one of those relatively new terms that was not an important factor in college admissions years ago. Now, however, its impact on your decision can actually be enormous, particularly at some schools. The term *"Demonstrated Interest"* means, "How interested are you in attending our institution IF we choose to *Accept* you?" NACAC provides an annual, extensive State of College Admission Report where you can read about the changes and trends in college admissions.

The first thing you need to understand is that the single most important statistic to a college is its *Yield* number. Say that 100 students apply to a school and the school *Accepts* 70 of them. The percentage of those 70 students who actually choose to attend is the school's *Yield*. This number is so significant to colleges because they want students to Attend if *Admitted*. Among the Internet, Common App, and other resources that evaluate colleges, more students are applying to more schools, even if it's "just because" their friends are applying or because they feel they have a good chance in admissions or because it's a college with no additional essays/fees. It makes sense, then, that <u>colleges need to differentiate</u>

between which students really are interested in attending and which students won't care much if they receive an *acceptance* letter.

> **A** It annoyed me when my friends shared that they had applied to a certain college but couldn't care less about being *Accepted*. If it was a school that I was considering attending, I found it frustrating that people would apply there "just because."

According to an article in *Inside Higher Ed* called "Pressure to Build the Class: 2016 Survey of Admissions Directors," 50 percent of colleges did not meet their projected *Yield*.

I'm generalizing information here, but typically the *Demonstrated Interest* factor does not apply to Ivy League, top-tier, and big state schools. Ivy League schools do not have to worry about their *Yield* numbers because they can feel confident that students want to attend their institutions if given the opportunity. State schools have the benefit of relatively low tuition, and many students attend in-state schools because they want or need to pay less for a college education. State schools also have such large student body populations that they simply do not have time to "track" students who are visiting or Demonstrating Interest. Although it's nice to sign in during a campus visit, it's really not necessary at most enormous schools; feel free to explore the campus on your own if you are in the area.

> **A** I found that I learned a lot, though, from participating in formal information sessions and tours. There's only so much you can learn on your own without a guide who knows the school inside and out.

However, Demonstrated Interest sometimes weighs so heavily in admissions for smaller, private schools that I have had many cases of academically strong students who are *Accepted* into Ivy League schools but *Deferred* or *Rejected* from excellent private schools because they had not demonstrated their interest. Many colleges would actually rather *Reject* a top student <u>before the *student* can</u> <u>*Reject* the *college*</u>.

> **A** An example from my own experience: prior to receiving my Early Decision notification from Cornell, <u>I was *Deferred* from a</u> <u>midsize liberal arts school</u>. The fact that my grades and scores were above its average should have qualified the college as a *Likely School* for me.

A college can protect its *Yield* by *Rejecting* students who, based on their academic strength, likely would attend a higher-ranked institution. Demonstrating Interest pushes students to learn more about colleges before they choose to apply. Additionally, Demonstrating Interest is especially important for your *Likely* college options that track it.

Methods of Demonstrating Interest

- ▶ Visit campuses. (This only counts if you SIGN IN with admissions, register for a tour, and/or attend an information session.)
- ▶ When geographically feasible, visit the same school multiple times. (Think about it, this shows that you are incredibly interested in attending that institution.)
- ▶ <u>Meet with professors</u> in a subject area you know well, if it is applicable.

> **A** My mom always tells me that of course you should treat other people nicely because that's the right thing to do, but you also never know where you might encounter the same person again someday. <u>Maybe the professor you meet happens to be</u> <u>best friends with your admissions counselor</u> and puts in a good word for you.

Keep in mind you would want to be well prepared to ask questions about the department or research. Meeting with a professor without clear conversation goals could be wasting their time and certainly not a help in the process.

▶ <u>Sit in on a class</u> (thank the professor and <u>f</u>ollow up with an email).

🅰 In addition to Demonstrating Interest, you can <u>cite this class as evidence of why you love the school</u> in a "*Why*" supplement. I found that professors I met, either through class or by an appointment, were so welcoming and happy to meet with me.

▶ Sign up for an interview.
▶ Attend local college fairs and always take business cards from the representatives so you can <u>follow up with an email</u>.

🅰 Something my mom taught me is that admissions counselors will rarely remember the five-minute conversation you might have with them while at the fair because they meet literally hundreds of students each day. However, the <u>counselors will likely read your thank-you email</u>, so now you have a connection with a person who potentially makes your final admissions decision.

▶ Meet with <u>college representatives</u> when they are in your area or high school.

🅰 If, for some reason, you cannot attend (maybe because you have a big test that period), try to stop by the guidance office and grab the <u>representative's business card</u>. You can send a follow-up email to ensure him/her that you are interested in the institution.

▶ <u>Send personalized letters/emails</u> to your admissions representatives to let them know about new substantial accomplishments or honors.

This is something my mom made me do often (probably more than was necessary). Crafting these emails requires work and organization because they involve finding the right person to contact at each school and writing a coherent and informative email. Every time your name pops up in a representative's inbox, it's proof of your interest in the school. However, this is a balancing act because you don't want to annoy the representative by overdoing it.

Since you have filed an application, you could ask follow-up questions to admission officers. Be sure to check the school's website first to confirm the answer is not there.

For the colleges that really consider Demonstrating Interest heavily, they will literally track your interest in the institution. For example, the admissions office might have an electronic folder with your name, and a tally will be made each time you visit the college, connect with the admissions officer, or request information from the school.

 The emails got a bit annoying at times. There is so much filing paperwork involved with this process, but it's worth it.

Once you get your contact information (name and email) onto a college's "prospective student" list, the school may send you links and pamphlets that border on advertising as a means of helping you learn more about it. Although it may be hard to imagine, some colleges are actually tracking *if* you open each email, *if* you click on the links they provide, and *how long* you spend on the site.

 Personally, I find this creepy. However, even though this sounds annoying, I devised a strategy for myself: once a day, before I started my homework, I would open all the links in the emails on my computer and let them sit there for a while. Later, I would explore the web pages that actually interested me. Don't make the mistake of deleting emails after you are done with them;

instead, file each into an email folder for that college. Clearly, no one has time to spend all day looking at a college's website, but you really want to appear as interested in the school as possible.

This is crazy, yet believe it or not these small things can actually have an impact on your application when added together. Some of the communications do contain useful and interesting information so you should read through them, when you can.

CHAPTER 9

Visiting Colleges

One of the most overlooked aspects of the college process is the in-session visit. Visiting a campus is critical to alleviating stress, and can greatly contribute to a happy college journey. I had been visiting campuses for more than two decades, but taking Amanda to visit colleges—sharing the process with her—created an entirely new dimension as we tried to picture her at each school. Beyond that, Amanda and I had a tremendous time together when we traveled all over the country visiting schools. I realize that the travel expenses can add up quickly (I have a few money-saving tips at the end of the chapter), but visiting is definitely worth the cost. We had so much fun talking to students, prepping for interviews, and exploring different cities. <u>I felt incredibly lucky</u> to finally be guiding my daughter (both physically and emotionally) on her journey to college.

> She's not just saying it to be cute; <u>we did have a lot of fun.</u> If you think about it, visiting schools is like looking around at places you might want to live for four years, which is both overwhelming and exciting. Throughout our countless college visits, I felt as if I got a little taste of everything.

It may sound crazy, but I think that your first visits should include three colleges to which you do not think you will actually apply.

A I didn't know this when my mom booked our first college trips. However, I quickly learned to determine what was important to me on a college campus without the pressure of looking at my "dream" school (although at that point, I did not yet have one).

Here's why: if you are lucky enough to have visited colleges early in this process (maybe in 10th grade), your attitude and grades may shift a lot before you apply during your senior year. Don't get caught up in the "name-brand schools;" visit schools to just learn as much as you can about what it means to attend college.

A Mom, this is so much harder than you are making it sound. Lots of students want to come back from a college trip able to say that they saw the Ivies.
In reality, she's right. There are so many amazing schools that few people in your town might have heard of, but so what? That shouldn't diminish the school's appeal.

Visiting a city school, a rural school, a small private school, and a big state school will give you a sense of the vastly different offerings around the country. Start locally by driving to colleges near home.

You should also visit schools that you are likely to get *Accepted* to (*Likely Schools*). Remember, you may end up attending one of them. One of the issues that worries students most is the fear that they won't get into their dream school. And, yes, the reality is that if your dream is an Ivy League college, your odds are not great (statistically). Visiting Harvard is fine, but most people do not get admitted to Harvard, even with amazing grades and scores. It would be great if you could visit schools that are a notch or two below your academic tier. If you happen to love one or two of them, you've just found the *Likely Schools* for your college list. More than that, however, you have just reduced a ton of stress. Imagine falling in love with a couple of *Likely Schools* and not having to worry about *if* you will get into college. You will not only feel confident that you will be *Accepted* to a college, but that it will be a college you love. You'll probably not only get into the *Likely Schools*, but also qualify for merit money.

When Amanda visited a few *Likely Schools* and loved them, it was a game-changer for both of us. I knew she would undoubtedly be *Accepted*, and she was absolutely thrilled with each of them. A huge stress in the college process was removed because <u>we were confident that Amanda would get into several colleges that she had visited and loved</u>.

A I can't even explain to you how nice it was to be ecstatic about schools that I knew should *Accept* me comfortably. From private, liberal arts schools to state schools and their honors programs, <u>I had options that I loved and was excited about</u>. For example, I applied to a big state school in the South that hardly anyone from my area attends. The school is in the middle of the cutest little city, and it offers a phenomenal education—especially the Honors Program to which I applied. This program *Accepted* me even before I heard from Cornell, and the security of this option in my back pocket gave me so much confidence.

It is very common for students to set their hopes on one specific school. However, if you remember that you need to find only a few colleges that will likely *Accept* you out of the nearly 4,000 to choose from, it turns the college process from highly stressful to far more enjoyable.

If you decide to prioritize visiting, you should try to visit each campus when that school is in session. Visiting during the summer, during Christmas vacation or Thanksgiving break is almost pointless. If you are across the country on a family vacation and want to visit colleges nearby during the school's break, of course you should do that because it is more convenient than coordinating a separate trip. The summer is certainly easier to schedule an interview and some colleges do have current students on campus. But <u>don't be fooled into thinking you understand the culture</u> of a particular campus if hardly anyone is there when you go.

A Truth. When our family took a vacation to California during Christmas break of my sophomore year, we visited three amazing schools that I *thought* I would love, but it was impossible to tell for sure. <u>You really can't get a sense of the social scene or type of kids who attend each school when the students aren't there.</u>

Seeing a campus while classes are in session is vital. Although attending an informational presentation and tour is great, there is a lot more to be gained when planning a visit. Remember that the <u>tours are often scripted</u> and given with the intent to "sell" you on a particular school.

A Something my mom taught me that I found really helpful is the advantage of walking next to the tour guide for at least a portion of the tour. While the tour guide will give the group lots of information while walking, he/she will often take a break when going inside a building or walking from one place to another. You can ask the tour guide some personal questions if you are up front, and <u>inquire about the things that interest you specifically.</u> For example, I would ask tour guides about the Greek Life on campus and the level of student spirit.

There is nothing wrong with that, but you need to investigate a bit further to learn more about what each college offers. Certainly, one tour guide does not necessarily represent the campus culture.

Many families try to visit up to four colleges in one day—this is too many. To really get a sense of each school—the academics, the campus life, and the students—you need several hours at least; plan to <u>spend a minimum of four hours</u> on a campus.

> ▲ More time if you can! It's nice to have an entire day to fully experience the school.

After your info session and tour, you will want to have a meal or snack in a heavily populated dining hall. In addition to testing the food for variety, accommodation, and taste, you will get a read on specifically who attends this college. Yes, this may sound superficial or judgmental, but remember that you are visiting colleges for *fit*. It is essential that you think you will fit in with the students who attend, and you can only make that call after observing the students firsthand.

> ▲ Pick a spot to eat where you are surrounded by several conversations, and try to listen to what is being talked about. Are the students gossiping? Talking about stressful schoolwork? Telling stories? Talking politics? Since childhood, I have always been fascinated to hear the conversations of college students.

There is no right or wrong here, but if you are honest with yourself, you may have preferences as far as how you feel about the answers to some of these questions:

▶ Are students sitting by themselves studying or eating in groups? What do the groups look like?

▶ Are students looking at their phones or are they talking to one another?

▶ Are the athletes sitting in a separate area of the dining hall? (Sometimes they have equipment or wear team identification.)

▶ Are the students wearing sweats? Do they look like models from a J. Crew catalog? Something in between?

> ▲ For some reason, I really took note of how students dressed at the schools I visited. I remember one trip to a South Carolina private school in which all the students were dressed as if they

were attending a business meeting, and thinking how strange that was (my high school had no formal dress code and I was comfortable in leggings or jeans). I knew from the instant I saw the students in the cafeteria there that I would feel like a "New York outsider" at this school.

▶ Are there students from different ethnic backgrounds or do they all look alike?

Although the following advice sounds daunting, it is much easier to follow than it seems initially: approach a group of students and tell them you are a prospective student. In most cases, they will invite you to sit down to talk with them. If this happens, it is fantastic because you can ask questions that you could not ask on the tour.

A This is one of my favorite parts of visiting colleges. It is so much fun to hear about the daily routines and social scene at each school from friendly students. At most schools, everyone was so welcoming and eager to tell me why I should apply.

Freshmen are great, but they are typically very happy with college in general and don't yet know the "insider scoop." While it's great to talk with first-year students about why they chose their college and what they like and don't like, keep in mind that they have limited experience. However, it is a golden opportunity if you can talk with upperclassmen. You can ask tons of questions, such as the following examples:

▶ What is your major? Are the professors accessible? Do they offer extra help and office hours?

▶ Did you always get the classes you want? Were there many options?

▶ Have you encountered red tape? Have you had interaction with the administration?

▶ How many hours per day do you study? How tough is the academic load?

- Where did you go to high school? Were you prepared academically for college?
- Did anything surprise you academically?
- Where are you from? Where are your friends from?
- Did you join a sorority or fraternity? Are you happy with that decision?
- How spirited are the students? (Do they sport the school's apparel? Do they attend school sporting events? Do they actively root for the school's teams?)
- To what other schools did you apply? <u>Why did you eventually choose this school?</u>

A <u>You can learn a TON from asking this one question.</u> You'll learn about the student's priorities and what the few things were about a specific school that made it stand out. Especially because I initially had such a big college list, it was helpful to hear from other students how they narrowed down their options.

- <u>What clubs did you join?</u> Do you recommend them?

A This is another great question; make sure you take notes on what the students say. <u>Club names and descriptions come in handy when writing a "*Why*" supplement.</u> Also, it's good to seek out as much information as possible about unique opportunities at each school—this also provides great essay-writing material.

- What don't you like about the school? What do you wish were different?
- Do you and your friends travel into the city nearby?
- Other than attend parties, what do students do on the weekends at night? What night of the week does the weekend typically begin?
- What if you don't drink or use substances? What are the options?

- Is the classroom vibe more collaborative, or is it primarily competitive?
- If you have enough time, <u>sit in on a class or two</u>, preferably in your intended major area.

> **A** This part is fun as well. You don't have the pressure of having to take a test on the material, so <u>you can really absorb not only the class's content, but also the classroom environment</u>. For example, I noticed at one school how much I could potentially thrive from a small class in which everyone knew each other. Also, it is exciting to be a visitor in class because, from my experience, the students are so happy to tell you about the class itself and answer any other questions you have. One girl in the Midwest even gave me her number after class and said I should text her with any more questions; she was so personable.
>
> In an intimate philosophy class in the South, the teacher instructed the 20 students to pair up and discuss the questions they had worked on for homework. I was sitting between two guys who eagerly invited me to listen to their conversation, which I found intriguing. The point is, students are usually so happy to have visitors. The professors I've met have been incredibly welcoming as well.

After class, follow up with students sitting nearby and ask them questions about their experiences. Thank the professor before you leave, and be sure to email a thank-you note after your visit.

Meeting and chatting with professors is an incredible way to learn about the education you will receive on a particular campus. I typically instruct my students to read about different professors within their intended major. If the professors have done research or written books, students should see if any of their work interests them. If it does, this is a perfect opportunity to reach out to professors before your visit and mention their work. Tell them when you will be on campus and that you would love to meet them. If the professor responds and is happy to meet with you, this will tell you a lot about the type of school and its access to the teaching staff.

<u>Be prepared, ask questions, talk about specific classes</u>, and always follow up with a thank-you email.

> **A** Meeting with a professor definitely requires homework. You'll want to be well informed about the academic opportunities at the school, yet still have thoughtful questions that demonstrate your curiosity. <u>Spend 20–30 minutes prepping for each meeting.</u>
> At one of my top schools, I met with two creative writing professors. I actually stayed in touch with them during the months that I applied to college, and it was special to communicate with respected individuals at that school.

Spend time exploring campus on your own and pay attention to what students are doing. Go into the career center and ask questions about internships and job help. How much can students earn? Do companies typically recruit for a particular job major? What percent of students graduate in four years and are immediately employed? See if students are utilizing the services and how helpful the staff seems to be.

Pay attention to bulletin boards. What kinds of events are happening? Also, definitely <u>grab a copy of the school newspaper—</u> it can give you a great sense of the activity on campus.

> **A** Especially because I worked on the staff of my high school newspaper, <u>I was interested in seeing what the college papers were like.</u>

Always schedule an interview if the college offers one. I'll talk more about this in Chapter 15, *Interviewing*, but wanted to remind you that an interview can be an integral part to the visit.

Having been a college counselor for more than two decades, I have noticed a huge change in the scene as students and their families sit waiting for their tours, interviews, or information sessions. It used to be that most people would talk to one another, ask from what cities or states other people traveled to arrive at the college, and how their college search process was progressing. However, similarly to many other areas of life now, people have their heads down—looking at screens. I gently suggest that you resist this temptation; be present and engage with other people in the waiting room of any admissions office. You can learn so much about the campus culture by talking to other high school students who are considering it as well. Where are they from? Are they visiting other colleges in the area?

> **A** If you have already read Chapter 20, *Keep Your Mouth Shut,* you might worry that my mom's suggestion that you share this information with others is contradictory to my suggestion *not* to share this information with your peers. Have no fear. This is one of the best parts about visiting colleges: no one knows you. You will likely never see the other prospective students again; the likelihood that you both end up at the same college is so very slim, and even if you did, you probably won't remember each other. Feel free to tell strangers where else you are visiting. I found that this was a great way to get some "college talk" off my chest while still protecting myself from the gossip circles of my own school.

What do they want to study? When I was once speaking to families at a small liberal arts college in Maine, I was blown away by the fact that 8 out of the 10 came from different parts of the West Coast. That school in Maine only has a few hundred people in each class!

Plan to check out the local town or city too. Choosing a college involves so much more than merely deciding what classes to take. Do you feel safe in the college's surrounding area? What is the security like? Are there shops? Restaurants? Does the local community seem to enjoy and support the college? If the college has access to a city, how often do students actually go downtown?

I strongly recommend that students use the app called Evernote (or something comparable) when visiting schools so they can take photos and notes in the same place. This makes it easy to refer back when writing an essay/supplement.

A Don't underestimate the importance of taking photos and notes about your thoughts and reactions as you visit a school. These documentations are SUPER helpful. When it was time to write my supplemental essays and answer questions such as "Why do you want to come to this school?" I was infinitely thankful that I had taken such thorough notes at each college. Notes will allow you to be very specific in your writing, and are another way to demonstrate your obvious interest. Also, if you visit enough schools, their programs and campuses will blend together in your mind and prevent you from being able to picture each individual school as clearly. Pictures to go along with your written thoughts are essential.

As a general rule of thumb, you do not need to spend nearly as much time visiting the state school campuses. For the most part, the state schools are too busy and too big to "track" which students visit. You do not have to register with admissions (although it is nice if you can). However, most of the private schools will be following your interest in them. If you take a tour or attend an info session, that information may be used as Demonstrating Interest and may help you during the admissions selection process.

A Some schools will actually have a section of their applications requiring you to check boxes denoting things you have done to Demonstrate Interest. Be able to check several of them.

If you are considering applying to a college through Early Decision (more in Chapter 17 on *Assessing Types of Applications and Responses*), I recommend a lot of extra visiting. Because Early Decision is a contract requiring that you attend the school if you are admitted, I feel better when students have done their "homework": my recommendation if applying Early Decision is that you visit at least 10 to 12 colleges in session prior to mid-October of senior year. In a perfect world, you would return to your top Early

Decision contender(s) two or three times, preferably including an overnight stay.

Clearly, the entire process can be very expensive, but please do not underestimate the importance of visiting colleges. Some schools will help foot the bill if you are a top student, while others may give you a fee waiver when you apply. Amtrak coupons for 11th and 12th graders make visiting colleges a bit more affordable. The company offers a "buy one, get a second one at 50% off" deal to juniors and seniors who visit colleges. I get a link through one of my professional memberships for my students, but anyone can get a similar discount through Amtrak directly amtrak.com/buy-one-get-one-50-off-with-college-campus-visit. Additionally, if you know some students on campuses you are visiting, you can ask to stay with them instead of at a hotel.

A Staying with students at their school is so much fun. You'll immediately get a sense of the daily routine at a school by living there, even if it's only for one night. Especially if you stay over a weekend, you'll also get a great taste of the social life.

Sometimes colleges will offer you a dorm room, too, depending on your circumstances. If you must stay in a hotel, check with the colleges you are visiting, as they often have significantly discounted arrangements for visiting students. There are also companies that offer group discounts to students who visit colleges. That seems to be a relatively new business and many students enjoy seeing several colleges that way. Some universities will offer fly-in programs to subsidize expenses of prospective students who demonstrate financial need. Although you certainly want to visit colleges while they are in-session, if you are on a budget, try to avoid busy dates such as Homecoming because hotels routinely increase their rates for special weekends. Finally, ask the admissions office if the college gives out fee waivers for students who take a tour. This is another growing trend, and while it only amounts to less than $100 per application, it's still nice to save that for other college-related expenses.

Remember, visiting should be FUN!!! I know I'm biased, but I think it is one of the most pleasant ways to spend a day. Having visited hundreds of colleges throughout the years, I love talking to the students and learning what they love (and don't) about their college experiences. For you, there should be no stress when visiting because it's like window-shopping: you are browsing with no commitment. The visits are the time you can start to form opinions about factors such as city proximity, Greek life, class size, school spirit, professor attention, and so forth. As you begin to develop preferences, you'll be able to formulate your final college list.

Jill's and Amanda's Dos and Don'ts When Visiting Colleges

DO	DON'T
Ask a lot of questions.	Be shy or nervous. Students will be excited to talk to you.
Be bold! Introduce yourself to students.	Leave after only an hour or two.
Attend classes; meet with professors.	Make judgments too quickly.
Spend time simply observing students.	Sit in the back of an information session or walk in the back of a tour group.
Get a good night's rest before your visit, and have your questions ready.	Worry if a particular school is not for you. It's important to identify the specific characteristics at the schools that you do not like.
Take lots of notes and pictures!	Get your heart set on only one school.
Eat on campus.	Daydream or space out. You need to soak it all in.

CHAPTER 10

Making a College List

After visiting a few college campuses and using the app Evernote, try to identify key characteristics that you absolutely must have or don't want in your ideal school. I usually allow my students five "must-haves." Sometimes, these factors are things such as the college dining halls must have delicious food, or that the professors must be available and accessible to students. <u>Must-haves can be absolutely anything that will make college the right match for you</u>—no judgment!

 When my mom told me that one of her own criteria for choosing a college many years ago was that it had semi-private bathrooms, I did judge her a little bit. ☺ I'm kidding—to each his/her own. I can totally understand where she was coming from, though. <u>To some people, a college's appearance matters a great deal; to others, not so much.</u>

Most students include solid academic programs as a large part of their criteria, but <u>your five "must-haves" can be whatever you want.</u>

 Here were my college "must-haves." All schools on my list had the following:

- Strong majors and departments in English, psychology and creative writing. At the time of formulating my list, I wasn't quite sure of what I would list as my intended major, but I knew that I cared about these subjects a lot.
- The option of Greek Life. Although I was not sure if I would rush, I wanted to have the choice to do so if I wanted.
- School spirit. Though a college did not have to have traditional rah-rah attendance at football games necessarily, in tenth grade, I was really struck by how many students were proudly sporting a Pennsylvania school's apparel. What I qualify as "school spirit" is students who feel passionately about their classes and activities, and a student body that is somehow united in one or more ways. There were definitely a few schools on my list that have Division III sports, but those schools perhaps have a different kind of spirit. Most colleges to which I applied have a somewhat bigger sports program because I am drawn to spirit.
- Campus. None of the schools on my list are city schools. All have a campus and the "quad scene" that I wanted and pictured for college.
- An overall friendly and welcoming feel among students. At one very competitive school that I visited in the South, students seemed overworked and mostly stressed about their college lives. I knew that when it came down to it, I would not choose a place where students are not happy.

Creating this list ensures that your college list will be made up of only schools that you like. If a college does not have even one of these characteristics, you can go ahead and remove it from your list. Remember that you are selecting a handful of colleges from literally thousands—don't settle. The "must-haves" can be as serious or as silly as you want. If, for example, you are applying with a 92 GPA and an ACT score of 29 and your criteria include the opportunity to study computer science, 5,000 to 8,000 undergraduates, having a Greek Life option, participating in discussion-like (smaller) classes, and four-year graduation rates above 70%, you can then immediately rule out hundreds of schools. However, these are appropriate "must-haves," and you can certainly make a long list of colleges that encompass all of these factors. Remember, you need to "shop" for colleges. It will take a while and your interests will likely evolve, but it's all good. Try not to let the enormity of the task overwhelm you, and if you have a good school counselor, he/she could be the best expert you know to help guide you!

Initially, most students and families consider geographic location: how close to home do you want to be?

A This was actually not a factor for me. Having become accustomed to living away from home after several summers at sleep-away camp, I did not want to choose a school based on how often I could come home. Though it turns out that I will be at a school only five hours from home, I strongly considered schools across the country.

Another basic factor to consider is the size of the college. How big do you want your classes to be? Some colleges pride themselves on keeping classes super small, like 10 to 12 students. At other institutions, you could be in class with hundreds and hundreds of students, particularly in an introductory level class. Do you want to attend school in a locale with a particular type of weather/climate? If you attended a public high school, is it okay if a lot of students at your college come from private schools? Of course, finances will certainly come into play, but if you are a relatively good student, please do not turn away from a school simply because of a scary sticker price. As long as students and parents discuss in advance how much your family will/can spend on college tuition, I strongly recommend that you apply to colleges that may be beyond your financial capabilities. I have had students receive free rides, half tuition, and many other deals; you won't know how much money a college will offer you unless you apply. However, if you apply to schools beyond what you can afford, it is a good idea to seek admittance to a few extra schools within your financial range in case you do not get the amount of merit money you had hoped (more on this in Chapter 18 on *Procuring Financial Aid*).

I would also urge you to strongly consider at least one or two *Colleges That Change Lives*. These colleges are dedicated to the advancement and support of a student-centered college search process ctcl.org/. While there are dozens of other colleges that change lives, the ones in this consortium meet the founder's ideals and want students to search for the right fit beyond ratings and rankings.

The academic calendar can vary significantly from one college to another. Students may want to consider distribution requirements and/or structure of the curriculum when weighing options. At some colleges, students only take one class at a time. At others, students get a condensed winter break to take more classes or participate in an experience (internship, travel, and so forth).

When considering a major, some students will think they have it all figured out and others will have no clue. Let me tell you a little secret: the students who think they know exactly what they want to do with the rest of their lives are usually wrong. Of course, I have seen exceptions, but please do not stress about it. Look around at all the adults you know and ask them how many times they have changed their careers—you will likely be blown away by the answers.

You want to choose a direction to explore, so how do you start? I think it is a great idea to read through books or websites that list all college majors and make a list of those that may interest you. *The College Board Index of Majors & Graduate Degrees* bigfuture.collegeboard.org/majors-careers and *Barron's Profiles of American Colleges* amazon.com/Profiles-American-Colleges-2017 -Barrons/dp/1438006896 both include indexes organized by majors.

If you fall into the camp of students who have a very specific major in mind, please make sure that there are several other majors that interest you. It is important to have options within a university in case you change your mind. Sometimes students are actually best served at colleges where they are not the "typical" student. I remember visiting a school in the South with Amanda that is best known for its pre-med majors, and yet she absolutely loved it as an English-centered person. The personal attention and small classes in her areas of interest were more suited for her than the popular classes.

While I am on the topic of pre-med, keep in mind that getting into medical school is often an ambiguous aspect of this process. You may want to delve deeper and learn more about the students who indicate pre-med on their applications to assess how many of them actually apply to med school. Especially at the more selective schools, the reality check of inorganic and organic chemistry motivates lots of students to find other majors during their college careers. It becomes a "weeding-out" process: in order for a selective college to boast very high admission statistics for medical school, they cannot have too many students applying. A smaller pool of students with a strong aptitude in math and science (particularly at a liberal arts school) could have a better shot at admissions to medical schools, partially because the professors at these colleges work hard to ensure their applicants meet with success. If a college provides a medical school *Acceptance* rate, you may want to check if they screen out applicants with a weak chance.

Ideally, your list should include about 10 to 12 schools: four *Likely Schools* ("Likelies"), four *Target Schools,* and four *Reach Schools.* For every *Reach School* on your list, you must have at least one *Likely School* to balance it out. It is fine to have more *Likelies* and *Targets* than *Reaches,* but not the other way around.

Believe me, my mom really stays true to her word on this one. We had several encounters that went something like this:

Mom: "Amanda, you need more *Likelies.* There are so many *Reaches* and *Targets* on your list and I don't want to see you get burned."

75

> Me: "Fine. I'll apply to that *Likely School* also." (It's no wonder that my list turned out to be so long.)

I am okay with no *Reach* schools. A college being selective does not make the school a better fit for you. Sadly, every year I receive at least a couple of phone calls in April from hysterical parents of my neighborhood's top seniors. They tell me that their son or daughter had applied only to top-tier colleges and received zero *Acceptances*. In my 24 years of experience, this has never happened to any of my clients, but it is devastating to me that this does happen regularly. I triple-check that each of my students has enough *Likelies* on his/her list so that this is not an issue, and I am absolutely adamant about this issue in my private practice. School counselors are busy people and I know that they try to make sure all students have enough *Likely* options, but if your school counselor is overworked and cannot check final lists, it's essential that you do your own research for your list. In order for a college to be in the *Likely* category, you need to make absolutely sure that you are comfortably *above* the school's ranges for both GPA and standardized test scores. <u>Falling in the middle of a school's range means that it is a *Target School*, and not a *Likely*—they are two different categories.</u>

> **A** There were also several instances when I disagreed with my mom about what schools actually qualified as *Likely Schools* for me. She (rightly so) would always point out that even if my statistics technically fell at the top of a school's ranges, I had to consider the school a *Target* or *Reach* simply because I live in an area where many people apply to a particular school. While I may have gotten annoyed with my mom at the time, <u>I realize that listing so many true *Likelies* that I loved gave me confidence</u> throughout the whole process.

Using Naviance scattergrams (more on this later) can give you an idea of where you fall based on graduates from your high school.

In terms of how to compile your final college list, I suggest that you use a combination of resource books and websites. If you have close friends who are older than you, you can ask what they used. I think the most important part of forming your college list is visiting many schools.

A So true. How can you possibly know what you want your college to look like and be like if you have not been exposed to a variety of characteristics? For example, on a trip to the Chicago and Illinois area the summer before tenth grade, I visited my first city school that essentially had no campus. I remember that when the tour guide was trying to lead the large group across the street, I looked at my dad and told him that I definitely wanted to go to a school with a campus. For the rest of the tour, I liked the city aspect less and less. Although cities are amazing and provide incredible opportunities for college students, I would prefer that my college not be literally *in* a huge city. Especially having grown up in a suburban-bordering-on-urban area, I love green, open spaces; to me, it's one of the things that makes college, *college*.

That way, students can identify which characteristics they absolutely must have in a college, and then look for schools that have all of their "must-haves" within their geographic and financial range.

When you find and visit a college that you love, ask current students what specifically drew them to the school and where else they applied.

A I loved asking this question. At one of my most favorite college contenders, many students told me that they were choosing between that school and Cornell. I felt as if I really learned so much when they compared the two schools.

This is a great way to get ideas of other schools that likely have a lot in common with the one you like. Sometimes students apply to schools because the college is in a particular region or in their home state or a state that offers in-state tuition/reciprocity. But, again, stay true to your "must haves."

If you really feel that you need extra guidance, you can consult with something like the *U.S. News & World Report*, but I strongly discourage this. These types of lists lack clear alternatives for accurate and reliable information. There is so much that goes into the selection process that relying on these lists alone can be misleading. I prefer you use a resource such as the *National Survey of Student Engagement (NSSE)*, which studies comparable information. The *NSSE* assesses students' experiences and perceptions to help prospective college students find the right match. Each year, *NSSE* asks hundreds of colleges and universities to consider different learning activities. Please note that many colleges do not participate in the NSSE and others do not share their information publicly.

NSSE developed a free pocket guide to help students choose a college. You can pick one up from your school counselor.

Individual colleges have their own data available separately. For a look at aggregate data, you may find these summary tables helpful: nsse.indiana.edu/html/summary_tables.cfm. Below are the questions from the 2016 NSSE, reprinted with permission:

Academics

- ▶ How much time do students spend studying each week?
- ▶ Do courses challenge students to do their best?
- ▶ How much writing is expected?
- ▶ How much reading is expected?
- ▶ How often do students make course presentations?
- ▶ Do class discussions and assignments include the perspectives of diverse groups of people?
- ▶ Are students expected to use numbers or statistics throughout their coursework?

Experiences with Faculty

- ▶ How do students rate their interactions with faculty?
- ▶ How often do students talk with faculty members or advisors about their career plans?
- ▶ Do faculty members clearly explain course goals and requirements?
- ▶ Do students receive prompt and detailed feedback?
- ▶ How often do students talk with faculty members outside class about what they are learning?
- ▶ How many students work on research projects with faculty?

Learning with Peers

- ▶ How often do students work together on class projects and assignments?
- ▶ Do students help each other learn?
- ▶ How often do students work together to prepare for exams?
- ▶ How often do students interact with others who have different viewpoints or who come from different backgrounds?

Campus Environment

- ▶ Are students encouraged to use learning support services (tutors, writing center)?
- ▶ How do students rate their interactions with academic advisors?
- ▶ How well do students get along with each other?
- ▶ How satisfied are students with their educational experience?

Rich Educational Experiences

▶ What types of honors courses, learning communities, and other distinctive programs are offered?

▶ How many students study in other countries?

▶ How many students get practical, real-world experience through internships or field experiences?

▶ How many courses include community-based service-learning projects?

There are also many terrific online tools to help students with the process of making a college list. Here are a few that often get good reviews from my students:

▶ *My Majors*. While this website will help students determine what college major matches their interests, it doesn't always yield up-to-date results (mymajors.com).

▶ Here's another one from the College Board to assist with research about majors (https://bigfuture.collegeboard.org/majors-careers).

▶ I love *Barron's* for this type of research. There is a nominal fee to use the website (barronspac.com/index.cfm?anonymous&page=cs).

▶ *My College Options*. This will give you a suggested list of colleges based on a survey you complete (mycollegeoptions.org/college-search-by-major.aspx).

▶ Naviance. Discussed in greater detail in Chapter 14; offered in many high schools as a vehicle to link with Common App and a way to submit school records. I really like to use Naviance's scattergram function if your guidance office makes that available to you. Keep in mind that your high school must have an account with Naviance in order to gain access to the information about students in your school. Please note that depending on how often the guidance office in your high school updates the data, it can be more or less accurate. Also, some guidance offices input this data based on their official records. Other times, they rely on students to self-report statistics. Naviance does give you a sense of your chances of admission (based on numbers only) as compared to students from your high school who previously applied to the institution. The website will give you more specific and relevant information than national statistics (naviance.com/). Naviance does not, however, give you other important data like "hooks" the applicants might have had. One public high school in Westchester, N.Y., keeps a College Book that not only includes data found on Naviance but also identifies if the applicant is a recruited athlete or has legacy. This is an extremely helpful tool; if your guidance office keeps data like that, it is typically far more reliable about your chances of admissions from your particular high school than any other resource.

▶ *DIY College Rankings.* This is another tool that will help you to create a customized college list (diycollegerankings.com/).

▶ *Unigo.* A college research engine that also offers good articles and reviews from students (unigo.com/).

▶ *College Results Online.* This site offers subjective information on colleges' ability to fulfill financial need. Among general statistics, this website also gives you the four-, five-, and six-year graduation rates of each school (collegeresults.org/). More colleges actually report six-year graduation rates than four-year rates when giving tours and information sessions.

▶ *The Integrated Postsecondary Education Data System (IPEDS).* This offers terrific information on class size and faculty classifications, i.e., graduate students, TAs, professors, etc. (nces.ed.gov/ipeds).

Amanda's College List Evolution and Tips

Hi everybody! I wanted to provide a few of my own tips about creating a college list. Realize that the college process is a *process* for a reason—your list won't just produce itself for you in a matter of minutes. Creating a list of schools takes a long time, and if you do your research carefully, potentially several years.

I suggest using Evernote to keep track of your college list. I had several different notebooks: one for each college trip, and several for making and finalizing the list of schools to which I actually applied. Create a different note for each school, and whenever you visit or read *anything* about that college, jot it down. Those little tidbits of information and your reaction to them will be so helpful when you sit down to write your supplements. For example, so many colleges ask "Why" you want to attend their institution as their essay questions. Having pictures with your notes through Evernote will help jog your memory and help you remember how it felt to walk through the campus and talk to students.

Because you will grow and mature throughout high school so much, it's totally normal for your college list to change a lot (mine certainly did). For example, I went through a period of time during my sophomore year when I didn't think I was even going to apply to Cornell, let alone apply Early Decision. I initially thought that the school was too big for me—before I found the College of Human Ecology.

Start big. Even as late as June of 11th grade, I literally had 40 schools on my list and didn't want to part with any of them. Because my mom wanted to make sure that I had enough *Likely Schools* on my list, every time I loved a school that was a *Target* or a *Reach*, she insisted that we add a *Likely*. So, how did I narrow my list down to 15 schools?

- Stay true to your "must-haves" and remember not to settle on a school that wouldn't be almost perfect (because nothing is perfect) for you.

- Contrary to popular belief (at least where I grew up), you do NOT have to apply to the same schools as your friends. In fact, you might feel a whole lot less nervous if you applied to several colleges that don't usually receive applications from people in your high school. And with thousands of options, my mom always recommends expanding your horizons.

- <u>Don't be lazy</u> and knock a school off your list simply because there is a challenging supplement question.

That so many students do this frustrates me. <u>If you think about how exciting it would be to attend a particular college, fill out its supplements</u>. It is absolutely worth your time. If financially it is too expensive for you, inquire about fee waivers.

Think about it: you're going to give up an opportunity for four years of your life just to avoid sitting down for an hour to write an essay? It doesn't make sense; just tackle those supplements so that you have options.

I visited so many campuses throughout high school that I literally changed my mind about where I was applying Early Decision at least a dozen times—if not more. I loved so many different colleges. During spring break of my sophomore year, we visited a private college in Pennsylvania that I thought for sure would be *the* one. The school *barely* made my final list, eventually ending up at the bottom. This is just one example of how <u>it's completely fine and normal to change your mind often throughout the process</u> as you continue to learn more about yourself.

I love that! This was Amanda's journey to grow and learn about herself and what she wanted from college. <u>It was truly an exploration of self-discovery.</u>

CHAPTER 11

Recognizing College Criteria: What Do Colleges Consider?

In this chapter, I list some of the most important criteria that colleges consider when reading your application. If you would like quantifiable data, I suggest you read NACAC's State of College Admissions.

Academic

Rigor of High School Record

How many AP and Honors classes did you take?

> **A** This is something that you should preferably begin thinking about even as early as middle school. The truth is, <u>colleges care what high school classes appear on your transcript.</u> Make sure that you take the most challenging curriculum you can handle without overextending yourself, and try to stretch yourself in subject areas you tend to excel in.

Did you challenge yourself to the best of your ability during all four years of high school? Did you start out in easy classes and then become comfortable enough to take difficult ones?

What does your senior year schedule look like (having three free periods probably is not a good idea)? However, if you condense your schedule to allow time for a job or an internship, that is another story.

 You'll seem lazy. While clearly free periods are a valuable time to take a breather, eat, and relax, more than two a day is a bit excessive.

Did you take the hardest classes in subjects that interest you? Did you "slack off" as high school progressed?

Class Rank (if available)

Self-explanatory: the higher the better!

 My school actually doesn't rank; we only have a valedictorian and salutatorian.

Academic GPA

There are many different GPA scales: 4.0, 100-point scale, and others.

Did your GPA remain relatively consistent from year to year? Was there a huge dip or a huge improvement at any point?

 I'll admit that I stressed over my GPA, particularly in junior year, when I wanted to protect my strong academic history. I was constantly worried that if I didn't do well in one particular quarter, my GPA would decrease. However, realize that most classes will even themselves out. Also, because your GPA is composed of so many classes, it takes a lot to dramatically change your average. Just try your best without getting too caught up in trying to calculate your GPA all the time.

Standardized Test Scores

 See Chapter 5 on *Understanding Standardized Testing*, for more of my experiences!

ACT/SAT (Note: This is not a mandatory criterion for 950+ test-flexible schools.)
  Subject Tests (SAT IIs)
  AP Tests

Essay

Schools check for plagiarism, as most students have Internet access.

If a school has a *"Why"* supplement, admissions counselors will scrutinize this extra carefully.

I wouldn't skimp on the time you spend on your essay supplements. Think about it: this is one of the only times that you can literally write whatever you want to admissions counselors. Essays are huge opportunities to expose the best of yourself. For example, in each essay for every college to which I applied, I tried to incorporate a few important points that lent insight into my personality: Key Club activities, my camp counselor experience, and my religious background to name a few.

If a college has an optional essay, you should definitely write it!

I tried not to judge people who decided not to write the "optional" supplements. I mean, come on! If you were an admissions counselor and had to choose between two equally qualified students, would you take the one who wrote the essay or the one who did not?

Recommendations

Colleges are looking to ensure that students submit letters from school counselors and teachers, and/or optional letters (if requested). Follow specific colleges' instructions.

Nonacademic

Personal Qualities/Characteristics

How would others describe you? How would you describe yourself? It is no coincidence that many colleges actually require you to answer this question on applications—colleges are looking to create a community. Each school tries to form a distinct culture.

Your character should come across in your essay, letters of recommendation, and "anything else" section of the Common App.

Make sure your writing style and tone reflect you positively.

Many colleges are looking to create a microcosm of society and seek to have a sprinkling of all different kinds of students. Colleges not only consider different religious and ethnic backgrounds, but also personality types and views (for instance, sexual orientation if you have an interesting story, liberal and conservative viewpoints, and so forth).

Interview

Make sure you are on top of this early—interviews will book up!

Prepare for interviews by reading about the college, its specific programs and opportunities, and clubs you may want to join.

<u>Dress nicely and professionally.</u> Business casual is appropriate. No necktie needed for boys. Girls do not need a dress or suit.

> **A** Depending on the school and whether I were dressing for an admissions interview or an alumni interview, I would wear either a sweater and jeans (put together, but casual) or a dress, similar to what I would wear if attending religious services. I never wore heels so I wouldn't have to think about tripping. <u>When in doubt, you can never go wrong with the "Dress to Impress" approach and wear something a little nicer.</u>

<u>Give your interviewer a firm handshake, a smile, and the best of your personality.</u>

A This is another circumstance when colleges really get to know you as a person instead of as unidentifiable statistics. I remember that when I had an alumni interview for a small school in Pennsylvania, the woman and I got along really well and had a fantastic conversation. I could tell that regardless of what my application looked like on paper, she was impressed by my personality and friendliness.

Extracurricular Activities

See Chapter 3 on *Choosing High School Extracurricular Activities*.

Talent/Ability

Hook (see Chapter 12 on *Hooks and Ways of Enhancing Your Application*).

Some programs require or recommend a portfolio for applicants (athletes, artists, and sometimes others).

Even if you hope to attend a college for one particular aspect (for example, playing a sport), make sure you would still love to attend that school even if you were not *Accepted* into the sports program or if you were injured and could not play.

First Generation

If neither of your parents attended college, you are considered "First Generation," which is advantageous because usually these students have a leg up on other applicants.

Schools love to give preference to students who are the first generation in their families to attend college. The assumption and rationale here is that students who grow up in an educated home are expected to attend college, whereas first-generation students might not necessarily have had the same expectations.

88

Alumni Relation

You are considered "Legacy" at a school <u>attended by one or both of your parents</u> at the undergraduate level.

> **A** But <u>don't apply somewhere just because your parents went there</u>. I always think it's crazy when one of my friends wants to go to a particular school simply because their parents attended.

A few colleges consider grandparents, aunts, uncles, and siblings as well.

Having a parent or close family member who attended a top-tier college could give you a bump in admissions and is considered a "hook." Typically, colleges are looking for children of legacy to have the grades and scores that the rest of the college community has attained. Often, these top colleges are inundated with qualified and overqualified students, and legacy can help with admissions at that point.

Geographical Residence

Are you applying to a state college within your own state?

It is sometimes more difficult to get into a state school that is out of your own state. Full-pay students often have an advantage in these cases.

Where you live can be a substantial factor in the admissions process. Working with so many students from the New York and tristate area, I am often asked, "How will my very bright, hard-working and accomplished ninth-grader get into a top-tier college?" While that potentially could happen, I tell families to move far, far away. ☺ If you live in an area like Long Island and your main objective for your child is to attend an Ivy League or other top-tier institution, you are living in the wrong place. I joke with these families that they should move to North Dakota, for example. Top-tier colleges are not getting nearly as many applicants from that state, so any one student's chances are dramatically improved.

Because there are so many wonderful and qualified applicants, colleges will want to create balance with students from a variety of states and countries.

State Residency

For state colleges, a huge admissions factor is dependent upon the designated percentage of students who must come from the home state. This percentage varies considerably from state to state and school to school.

Accepting out-of-state students increases tuition dollars, which greatly helps colleges. However, state schools are supposed to be loyal to their own residents first. The percent of students a particular college must *Accept* from its own state varies widely from one institution to another. The state you reside in affects admissions in the case of all state colleges and universities.

Religious Affiliation/Commitment

Generally, this is not a big factor in admissions. The exceptions are for colleges that are religious in nature and looking for students who share and embrace that faith.

For universities looking to create more diversity, they may take interest in a student who has a particular religious background that has shaped his/her life and maybe chose to write about this in an essay.

Racial/Ethnic Status

Colleges clearly try to build diversity within each class. While you cannot control this factor, it is something to consider.

Volunteer Work

Even if your high school does not require it, <u>do it</u>. Volunteering is important regardless of college.

 My high school actually did not require any community service at all, but <u>I was authentically involved with it through Key Club</u>. And I wrote a lot about these experiences.

However, like any other activity, if you dig deep and have a sustained commitment to volunteering, this will be a plus as far as college admissions. Having leadership roles in volunteer-oriented activities can also be helpful.

You do *not* (and probably *should* not) have to travel overseas to do volunteer work. Help out your own community first.

Work Experience

Work experience shows dedication and responsibility.

<u>Can your employer write a good letter of recommendation (LOR) for you?</u>

 <u>My boss at camp wrote one for me.</u> See Chapter 13 on *Getting Letters of Recommendation.*

Whether it is helping out with family expenses or just having a job to earn money for your own spending money, taking initiative to do work of any kind is a good thing.

If you must work to help provide extra money for your family's expenses, you should absolutely indicate that on your application. You are not at a disadvantage in the college admission process if you cannot play high school sports or join clubs because of financial restraints. All colleges understand commitment in support of family as a prime example of responsibility and maturity, important character traits in successful college students.

Work experience teaches you about life experiences, something colleges love to see.

Demonstrated Interest

See Chapter 8 on *Demonstrating Interest and "Playing the Game."*

Financial Ability

Your family's financial ability to pay could help or hurt you in the college admissions process (see Chapter 18 on *Procuring Financial Aid*).

While there are still some very wealthy colleges that are 100% need-blind, these schools are now few and far between. It is only a select group of colleges that can afford to take a student regardless of his/her ability to pay for tuition. The reality is that despite an admission officer's best intentions, reading through someone's application, the trained eye can surmise financial need (from zip code, parents' employment, etc.). To understand the complexity of this issue further, you may want to read this article: universitybusiness .com/article/colleges-lead-need-blind-admissions.

Students who are full-pay are in a unique situation: most students/families cannot pay for all of college. Many colleges that are need-aware look at students who can outright pay for all of college through a slightly different lens.

Social Networking

Clean up your Facebook and other social networking sites.

<u>Everything you have online should be able to be read by your grandmother</u>—that is the barometer to use.

> **A** A good idea is turning on Timeline Review on Facebook. In the case that one of your friends tags you in a maybe slightly inappropriate picture, it won't show up on your timeline. That said,

just be careful with what pictures are taken of you in general. Everything could end up online.

Simply Google yourself and see what comes up. Are there accomplishments and things you are proud to represent? In an age in which technology use is increasing, it is customary for some admissions counselors to Google their applicants' names in order to narrow down the pool. Make sure that you have nothing to be ashamed of.

CHAPTER 12

Hooks and Ways of Enhancing Your Application

Perhaps you are wondering how exactly to define a "hook." It is a term I use all the time with my students to describe a specific attribute they might possess that <u>separates them from most</u> (or preferably all) other applicants.

A My mom's favorite example is curing cancer. She loves to say that, "<u>unless you cured cancer</u>, you don't know for sure that you'll get into _____ college."

A hook is something that colleges are looking for in order to create a diverse, accomplished, freshman class. Colleges look for different hooks each year because they try, with each class, to create a microcosm of society. They want a well-balanced class. Very selective colleges do reserve about 17% to 20% of their class for recruited athletes, and colleges typically aim for 8% to 12% of the class to be minority students. Many liberal arts colleges are composed of one-third recruited athletes, and multicultural students can compose higher than 20% of a class. Anywhere from 10% to 15% of a class is usually made up of legacies. Some top schools also reserve a very small percentage of the class for development cases, defined as families who make very significant financial contributions to the university. The international students and students with special talents can add to these numbers even more. All these hooks combined can add up to half of an entire class.

Falling into any of the above categories (athlete, minority, legacy, development case) is considered a hook. However, <u>do not get overly confident</u> if you qualify as a legacy.

 As powerful as it is in college admissions to have legacy, <u>you need to first fulfill the school's requirements</u> before that will help you; legacy will distinguish you from your other classmates applying to the same school, but it will not make you a stronger student.

I have seen many students who think that because they have legacy at a certain school, they will definitely be *Accepted*. This is simply not true, especially if you live in a very populated, well-educated part of the country like New York. In order to "use" your legacy status, your best bet is to be a qualified candidate on your own merits from every angle. If your grades, scores, and activities align with the university's average or above average population, your legacy status could differentiate you from other students.

Do not despair if you don't have legacy at a top-tier school— most people don't have that. The reality is that you will either fall into one of the above categories or not: there is not much you can do about it. However, <u>there are many other opportunities to enhance your application</u>.

For example, I tried to <u>expand upon my extracurricular activities</u> as much as possible (more on this in other chapters).

If you have extreme talent in another area besides athletics, such as being a competitive musician or singer, your application will be helped as well. Colleges want to admit students who make an impact on their homes, schools, and communities. You do not have to be the president of a club, but how did you contribute to its growth and development? Admissions counselors reason that if you made an impact in high school, you are more likely to contribute to your undergraduate college community. While contributions to your high school community typically are not hooks, they can positively influence your life, your memories of high school, and your success in the college process.

Students constantly ask me what actions they can take in order to improve their chances of admissions. My answer is always "be authentically you." If you genuinely love to play the piano and have some talent, practice, enter competitions, and try to earn some regional, local, or national recognition. However, keep in mind that most students are not quite lucky enough to have a talent like this, and yet they will all still get admitted to colleges. I am only addressing the hooks not because you necessarily have one, but just in case you do and are not certain how to pursue it to make it help your application. The reason I try to focus on students being authentic is that <u>there are no guarantees in college admissions</u>— no matter what crazy, distinguishable hook you may have.

 She's right. To reiterate a theme we continue to mention, you should <u>participate in activities throughout high school that you will truly enjoy</u>, not ones that you *think* will get you into college.

Here are some things about enhancing your application via authenticity that I know for sure:

▶ <u>Authenticity resonates on applications</u> and in your life in general.

 It's true. <u>It is so much better to come across as *you*</u> on your application, instead of your trying to be someone else.

▶ Regardless of the outcome and which colleges admit you, you will have chartered a journey you loved and a process that was enjoyable if you stay true to your personality and passions.

▶ Even if your piano playing (or other talent) did not quite yield the results you were hoping for in college admissions, you will be a better musician (or whatever) from having practiced, and you will have enjoyed reaching new levels of achievement.

▶ Despite what most people believe, applying to college is not all about the final product (the college you eventually choose). If you *Love the Journey*, you cannot go wrong here. A very selective college may be looking for a talented pianist this year, but next year they may need an oboe player and have no need for another pianist. There is no way to anticipate this for a particular college years in advance. A part of your success in this process is luck and trusting that you will end up where you are meant to be.

Athletes

While being an athlete is fun and can give you a huge advantage at some colleges, I do think that <u>being a serious athlete who wants to play in college can mean double the work to apply</u>. Of course, I have worked with athletes who have had a pretty easy time in the college process.

A My best friend was recruited for lacrosse at a very prestigious, small, liberal arts school in July after junior year. I remember being thrilled for her because <u>she had worked so hard to be a stellar athlete and student at the same time</u>, but so jealous of her that she already knew where she was going.

Because these students are talented, coaches seek to recruit them early in the process. If an athlete receives a nice offer from a respectable school, the process is typically very smooth. More often, however, there are a few more kinks to work out. Most student-athletes work very hard in hopes of playing on an NCAA (National Collegiate Athletic Association) team, but sometimes this simply does not work out as anticipated. Your particular sport will determine how early the recruitment process begins. For the purposes of not overwhelming athletes and their parents further, I will explain the basics here:

If you are a high school athlete, rest assured that NACAC (National Association for College Admissions Counseling) does have guidelines that coaches, colleges, and players are supposed to follow. For example, colleges are expected to follow deadlines to prevent an open-ended process for student-athletes. Families need to understand from coaches and admissions officers that athletic scholarship offers do not guarantee a favorable admissions decision on behalf of the university. See nacacnet.org/news--publications/publications/get-into-the-gamr/ for more information.

There are three levels of NCAA sports, called Divisions I, II, and III. Division I is the highest level of intercollegiate athletics (Division I-A for football). These schools typically have larger budgets, more advanced facilities, and more athletic scholarship opportunities. Division II includes student-athletes who may be just as skilled as D-I but the D-II schools often have fewer financial resources. Division III schools do not offer scholarships but offer competitive sports at more than 400 colleges.

The Ivy League schools and other elite colleges use a formula called the *Academic Index* to determine minimum academic expectations for athletes. The AI is a score out of 240 based on the averages of standardized testing scores and class ranking (often not available) or GPA.

High school athletes should definitely sign up on the NCAA website during their junior year.

Seek help from your high school or travel team coach. Coaches often have relationships with colleges and can therefore assist in this process.

Try to determine which colleges are on your list based on academic merit and decide where you would like to play if given the choice.

Contact the Sports Information Director at each school. They should be helpful in finding the names of coaches and assistances. Each school has an SID. You should also connect with each coach with an emailed letter and résumé so that he/she knows you are interested in that particular college. It is helpful for coaches if you put together your own statistic sheet that includes identifying information such as your height, weight, etc. Also provide a list of athletic achievements and awards, as well as your high school grade point average and standardized test scores. Furnish any other relevant information that coaches can use to first look over your application profile. Often, coaches would like to see a video of you playing. However, keep in mind that the NCAA puts limits on the amount of contact coaches can have with those they are recruiting, including time of year and number of visits. Remember that for college purposes, you are a student first; therefore, coaches will want to see how you can hold up academically before learning about your athletic capabilities. It is true that many colleges hold their recruited athletes to a lower academic scale and criteria. Although seemingly unfair to non-athletes applying to selective colleges, the rationale is supposedly the following: because these students are spending so much time playing and practicing their sports, they have not been able to devote as much time to their academics as other students. Ideally, of course, because athletes are often capable of the same academic merit as other applicants, their sports can give them a significant advantage.

Hope for the best, but plan for the worst to ensure that you have a backup strategy in case the athletic component doesn't come together the way you want. Perhaps you get injured and will not be able to participate in college, or maybe you do not get offers from colleges that interest you most. It is important to have lots of options so that, ultimately, you get to make the best choice for you.

When you visit schools, ask members of the current team what it is like to play on the team for that particular coach. Does the coach care about them? What happens if you are injured? Remember, coaches are often also the team's recruiters. How they recruit and how they coach can be strikingly different, so learning the realities from the team is an excellent way to determine a good fit for you.

Students pursuing liberal arts colleges may be required by coaches to apply Early Decision to the school.

If you are a Division I or I-A prospect, you may either need a well-vetted travel coach or hire a specialized consultant who can help navigate the college athletic process.

Artists

Students interested in the fine and/or performing arts have two big options. There are professional degrees called a Bachelor of Fine Arts (BFA) or Bachelor of Music (BM), or they can pursue a Bachelor of Arts (BA) degree. BFA and BM degrees are offered in conservatory programs or specialty schools. In these programs, most of the coursework is specifically in art or music. But if that's not for you, there are many colleges that offer BA degrees in music, dance, fine arts, acting, etc., with the requirements to take classes in the arts usually being easier to handle.

If you have a special artistic talent, colleges definitely want to know about it as an example of how you spent your time during high school. However, unless you are applying to college as an Art major, you do not have to send a portfolio of your work.

I had a client who loved photography—his passion—but wanted to major in something unrelated. What he did was put together a collection of his favorite photos, which he kept ready to share with any college representative who happened to take an interest. He signed up for a few regular admissions interviews, and when his photography came up, he was able to share some of his work. So while the student did not submit the photos in any official portfolio, he managed to show them off to colleges. At one school, in fact, someone was so impressed that he asked for the student to send him the work electronically so he could share it with people in the art department and around the university. This is a perfect example of a student authentically applying to college: because of his interest in another pursuit, he was not forcing himself to be an art major. That said, art is still one of his passions, something he wanted to come across on his application.

If you do want to major in art, you will need to submit your portfolio as part of the admissions process; just like an athlete, this talent can be your hook. Typically, admissions counselors will share your work with the relevant faculty for their analysis. If you are applying to be a photography major, for example, your work will be analyzed by appropriate professors who will weigh in on what they think your chances are of success in their department. However, the admissions office will still be deciding whether you get into the university. If admissions wants to *Accept* you but the professors who study photography question your level of talent or ability, you may be admitted to the school without the major you wanted. Students should view college websites to learn about portfolio (and audition) requirements. Students may also want to visit portfolioday.net/ to get an assessment of their portfolios. Because of the variety of portfolio review and audition requirements, the admission calendar may be vastly different than for the nonartists.

Acting/Dancing/Singing (Performing Arts)

Similar to traditional artists, students who have a talent for acting, singing or dancing should certainly share this with colleges. However, whether this is a hobby or a career interest may dictate how to proceed in the admissions process. Many colleges offer auditions for talented students who are interested in majoring in one of these areas. If singing is just a hobby, however, that may just be a wonderful aspect of your extracurricular life with no bearing on your chances of admissions. You probably won't be able to share your voice with colleges during the typical admissions process without an audition. However, there are some exceptions and, similar to artists, you should plan to have a short demo available that showcases your vocal range and talent—just in case someone interviewing you asks to hear it. Some colleges will review a portfolio for a student not planning to major in art or a performing art.

If you are pursuing a major in one of these fields, sign up for auditions whenever possible and be prepared to showcase your talent.

In general, less is more when it comes to officially submitting art portfolios/videos that showcase your talent, if you are not applying to major in that area. Admissions staff members are very busy people, so you only want to highlight your best accomplishments when you submit your application. If you can ask art professors at specific schools about whether a portfolio is worth submitting, that is helpful. High school art teachers are often happy to help prepare them.

The "additional section" on the Common App is probably one of the most potentially beneficial, yet underused, aspects of differentiating yourself on your application. In most recent years, the Common App allows you to use an additional 650 words to write about literally anything you want. While some students may need to utilize this space to explain a mistake (such as an incident with the police or poor grades), most students have the opportunity here to highlight something special. For example, explain how you overcame a learning disability or go into greater detail about one of your extracurricular activities. If you have been involved with something for three or four years, hopefully you would have more to say about the impact you have made than the initial 150 characters allowed in the activity section of Common App. Many students come to me with what they think is a completed application, yet the extra section is often blank, and I instruct them to fill it. While you do not want to use that section to reiterate what can be found elsewhere on your application, you do want to explain, expand, or delve deeper into something if it is appropriate.

If you have a documented learning disability (LD), you must understand that the accommodations and services required by secondary schools will not necessarily be available after high school. If you will want to continue those accommodations and services, you will first need to make sure that the colleges to which you are applying provide them and then decide whether to disclose your circumstances on your application. Contacting the college's Learning Support Center (rather than Admissions) is appropriate. If you have a LD, your best bet is to speak with your school counselor or another trusted mentor who knows your situation and understands the laws surrounding students with disabilities, in order to make informed decisions in this process.

CHAPTER 13

Getting Letters of Recommendation

Believe it or not, letters of recommendation (LOR) can have a tremendous impact on your admission chances, if you seek out the right people and if you apply to schools that carefully read them.

The following is a blanket statement that may not apply to all schools, but larger state institutions often cannot take the time to read letters of recommendation. If you are assessed as being in the "gray area" after your application is reviewed at a large school, a solid LOR can make the difference. In the past few years, I have noticed that many larger schools actually tell students that they should not send LOR unless they are applying to specific programs that request them. This is a new trend with some of the top colleges in the University of California (UC) system especially. If you are applying to smaller schools, however, your LOR will usually be read multiple times and will be weighed a considerable amount.

Clearly, I will focus more on the colleges that ask for letters in this chapter. Some colleges require as many as four LOR and as few as none. In the past, I advised students to send as many strong letters as they could. However, this would be horrible advice today. Whether this is sad or just a reality, the fact is that many colleges are overwhelmed. Admissions counselors want what they want—nothing more. While there are certainly exceptions, and often students can read between the lines of a college's LOR policy, my advice is simply to follow the guidelines. For example, several top-tier colleges now request only one school letter (typically school counselors write these) and one letter from an academic teacher. Though they will allow you to send extra letters, they want only those two.

Many colleges require just one "school letter," which many students will have their school counselors fulfill. With the growing number of caseloads counselors have, colleges will now accept the school letter from anyone employed by the school, but I still prefer the school counselor when possible. First of all, you hopefully have worked throughout high school to have a relationship with him/her for four years. <u>Go out of your way to talk with your counselor</u> about different classes or opportunities you are considering (see Chapter 6 on *Staying Proactive and Starting Early*).

 I also commented more on <u>this</u> in that chapter. ☺

Little interactions will hopefully eventually translate into a solid letter of recommendation. Typically, although I know I am biased, <u>school counselors are genuinely good people</u> who want to advocate for you.

 My high school guidance counselor is so compassionate. I think <u>she really tries her best to assist all her students</u> in whatever way she can.

However, they are often super busy and handling triage all day. Because their caseloads have increased, sometimes the college counseling aspect of their jobs gets put on the back burner. Nevertheless, you can always advocate for yourself: as you start some research and learn what you want and do not want in a college, make an appointment to share what you have learned with your guidance counselor. Generally, most counselors enjoy what they do and are especially <u>impressed with students who take initiative</u>; they will want to help you in whatever way that they can on your journey to college.

> **A** My school counselor was impressed when I came into her office with specific questions about a certain college's programs or information I had found in a book or online. I've found that <u>adults are impressed by students who engage in learning outside of school</u>—even if the topic is colleges.

From my experience in listening to several information sessions recently and having the chance to speak with admissions counselors, I have learned a few things about LOR submission. We already know that many people who work on a college's admissions staff are overworked and tired of reading extra material. Additionally, both the top-tier and smaller colleges will typically read everything you send them. Therefore, if you send one teacher letter that is phenomenal and a second that is just pretty good, you really only want schools to read the first letter. This is an important distinction because, as much as amazing letters can set you apart from the applicant crowd, letters that are merely "okay" will make your reader's eyes glaze over. Whether to send any letters beyond the number a college requires should be very well thought-out; <u>you want admissions counselors to read only the very best</u>. And, of course, you must adhere to the limitations imposed by each institution.

> **A** I applied to most colleges with an intended major in English, and it would make more sense for my "number one" letter to be from an English teacher. So, <u>I respectfully requested that my "second" teacher *only* submit to a few schools</u> that either specifically requested two teacher letters or schools that I thought might take time to read a second teacher letter (smaller schools).

You will be asked to decide about the confidentiality of your letters. The law that affects this is called the *Family Educational Rights and Privacy Act* (FERPA). Many applications give students an option to waive their right to view their LOR. If looked at from the college's perspective, I would highly recommend that students sign this form. If a student asks a teacher to write him/her a letter but does not trust that it will be good, why would the student ask in the first place? Waiving your rights tells your teachers and admission counselors that you are confident about your letters and do not need to see them. Understand that even if the FERPA form is signed by a minor, it is legally binding. Also, once a student signs a waiver, it applies to all recommendations for all colleges.

So, how do you go about choosing the teachers to write your LOR? The ideal writer is someone who had you as a student in an academic class in your junior or senior year—and perhaps additionally as an underclassman. If the teacher is also the advisor of a club with which you are involved, that person becomes an even better choice. Most importantly, you want a teacher whose subject makes sense or aligns with your "intended major," and <u>who knows you well</u>.

A My first teacher was easy for me to pick: I had her as an Honors and AP English teacher in ninth and eleventh grades; she is the advisor of the school newspaper for which I had leadership and editorial positions; I did an Independent Study with her in creative writing in tenth grade; she taught the subject of my intended major at many colleges; and, most importantly, <u>I knew that she could speak of me as both a hardworking student and a good person.</u> For my second letter, ultimately, I decided to ask my Spanish teacher. I had her as a classroom teacher in ninth and twelfth grades, and I did a Conversational Spanish Independent Study in eleventh grade when a typical Spanish class did not fit into my schedule and I wanted to work more specifically on my speaking skills.

I would much rather you seek a letter from a writer who knows you well and taught the class for which you received a "B" than a teacher who barely knows you but gave you an "A." Some colleges will specify the subject areas for teacher recommendations if you are applying to particular programs.

When do you drop the question? The spring of your junior year is the ideal time to make an LOR request. For the most part, by the spring, teachers are finished writing for the current seniors, and they are not yet overburdened by the volume of letters they will be expected to write in the fall.

A This is important. There is a social studies teacher in my school that I know is a highly desired teacher in terms of writing LOR. My friends who waited until the fall of senior year to ask him were very stressed out because he could not guarantee them spots on his letter list.

I suggest that you take the time to meet with each teacher and ask him/her if he/she would write for you. If the teacher agrees, you should follow up by providing a "résumé" of interactions with him/her, special projects you completed, or other anecdotal experiences you shared together. This list will jog the teacher's memory about you as a student.

A For anyone planning to ask for a letter of recommendation, my English teacher actually had an "assignment" for which we had to discuss some character traits (supported by examples from class) we felt she could write about in a letter. So, she actually made the entire process a lot easier. For my Spanish teacher who did not give specific instructions, I provided a "résumé" of my Spanish studies and our interactions together, when I asked her to write for me.

For example, let's say you had been particularly active in the discussion about Shakespeare's *Macbeth* in your English class. You could mention this participation in your "résumé" for your English teacher. Although some may disagree, I do not think you need to give your "recommender teacher(s)" your real résumé of extra-curricular activities. That list might be helpful and appropriate for your school counselor, but your teacher should really just focus on you as a student and potentially as a club participant or leader if he/she is the advisor.

A Remember that colleges want to know what kind of student you are. I think you should save the activities for your school counselor to discuss. ☺ The worst thing that could happen is for your letters to overlap in terms of the information they discuss, and as a result bore your college admission counselors into *Rejecting* you.

What about the other letters? Students often get caught up attempting to determine who could write an "outside" LOR. The writer's title means next to nothing—it is all about the relationship the two of you have established.

A I toyed with asking a few different "outside" people because I am extremely involved with several groups and organiza-tions: I could have asked my clergy at my temple, my advisors of Key Club or Debate, or my theatre director. However, I ultimately decided upon one of my bosses at camp. This woman literally watched me grow up as a camper, successfully complete the camp's CIT program, and, finally, work there during the summer after 11th grade. My boss watched my countless interactions with eight- and nine-year-old girls, how I dealt with conflict, and how I overcame bunk struggles. Additionally (and perhaps most impor-tantly), her letter describing my work with children would align with my intended major at Cornell, Human Development.

I have had students say, "My uncle knows the president of such and such company, and he said that 'said person' would write a letter for me." When I ask how well my student knows this person, I get a shrug because often they have never even met. This is not a good writer choice for you; colleges want to get to know *you*. Colleges

109

<u>will simply not care that you know an executive or famous person</u>
<u>peripherally.</u>

> **A** I remember my mom once telling me a story about her client who wanted the governor to write a letter for her because she had once worked at his assistant's office. However, she had never even met this man; she was only connected to him through a long chain of "subordinate" workers. <u>How could someone possibly write a good LOR for you if that someone doesn't know you?!</u>

CHAPTER 14

Using Common Application, Naviance, Universal Application, Coalition for Access, and More

Sometimes you will have a choice about how to apply to a specific college, and sometimes you just have to use the one vehicle that each school requires. Nearly 700 colleges participate in the Common Application (commonapp.org) as of 2016 with the intention of making it easier for students to input and submit their information only one time for several colleges, thus simplifying the entire application process. <u>Common App is a fairly user-friendly application</u>, but it can get labor-intensive with all the colleges' supplemental questions and additional essay requirements.

 "User-friendly?" <u>That's debatable.</u> It depends on whether the Common App is in a good mood and functioning properly.

Sometimes, students believe that by using the Common App they will only have to write one essay when applying to college. Depending on where you apply, that is likely far from the truth: while it is true that Common App allows you to submit one "main essay" to several schools, <u>many colleges will have other writing suggestions and requirements</u>.

> **A** <u>I literally wrote over two dozen essays</u> in total for my college applications. While I sent my "main essay" to several colleges, the other essays are just as (if not more) important.

Typically, the more selective the college is, the more likely they will want additional essays or supplements. Common App has evolved over the years and the website has certainly had technical issues. However, in recent years, the process has gone fairly smoothly for Common App users.

This may all change with the launch of *Coalition for Access, Affordability, and Success*, an application that is new for the high school class of 2017—but that can be used with only select colleges. As of 2017, more than 100 colleges have joined. The Coalition's goal is to provide college access to underrepresented minorities and low-income students, but I have significant reservations about how this will develop. Basically, the Coalition will provide "lockers" that will serve as repositories for confidential materials uploaded by high school teachers and counselors. These items, which will include letters of recommendation, transcripts, etc., will be placed in "sealed envelopes," and while the students will not have access to the material submitted by recommenders on their behalf, they will be able to add and delete their own work and accomplishments (awards, recognition, and so on) as they please. Students will have the ability to submit the envelopes to colleges as part of the Coalition process.

For the most part, participating colleges in the Coalition also allow applicants to employ the Common App; however, a couple of colleges have become Coalition-exclusive. I should note that this is not the intention of the Coalition: one of its motivations behind creating a new avenue to apply to college is the need to create competition within the application industry. The Coalition believes that by being forced to think about college earlier, students who might otherwise be at a disadvantage will benefit. For example, if a student receives an award in ninth grade for a music competition, he/she could add the certificate to his/her "locker." This would enable students to organize their accomplishments throughout high school so that they can more easily create detailed résumés in twelfth grade.

My favorite aspect of the Coalition is the students' ability to invite any mentor to their locker. A coach, Independent Educational Consultant, and an outside teacher could all provide insights and advice, which is a nice update to the college process. Additionally, after all the data is updated, the process is completed. You have to enter it all only once, so you could presumably do this in tenth or eleventh grade and know that aspect of your application is complete.

It is still too early to tell how many students will use the Coalition, but there has been substantial money invested in the application. I think it is safe to say that the Coalition will exist for the next few years at least.

Another application type is hard to categorize because there are so many application vehicles specific to only one college. Typically, many state schools create their own applications. Rather than using and paying for something like Common App, state schools use these "other" applications, which are often very tedious and require significant detailed information beyond what is used for Common App.

A Here's a heads-up about the UC (University of California) application system: it is annoying! Make sure you have access to all your grades throughout high school, and move through this application slowly and carefully. The one good thing is that if you are applying to multiple UCs, you only need to complete this application one time and simply check off the boxes of which campuses interest you. It's not that the required details are difficult or particularly thought-provoking, but boy, are they time-consuming. You won't believe the volume of questions on some state applications, including asking about everything from what state your parents are registered voters to what grade you received in ninth grade art.

A number of state schools will actually allow applicants to choose between their own applications and the Common App. In this instance, it is often easier to use Common App, as you are likely using that for other applications anyway. By avoiding a state's specific application, you will not have to fill out all your preliminary information again.

 Yes! Always choose Common App!

There are 33 universities including Ivy and top-tier colleges that participate in the Universal College Application, which is struggling to survive as a relevant college application vehicle. The UCA does offer some valuable options so I would not count it out quite yet. First of all, it is quick to respond to questions and provide technical support. It has been on the forefront concerning gender identification questions and includes a question that accommodates the "new SAT." All applicants who submit through UCA must complete a required extracurricular short answer and an additional information space allows for résumé uploads. Additionally, the UCA system allows for tailored letters of recommendation. A paper version of the application is also available for students without Internet access.

Among other programs and websites, Naviance is a "college and career readiness software provider" that partners with high schools to provide students with college planning resources.

> **A** Because I visited so many schools, <u>I found Naviance most helpful when viewing scattergram charts</u>. Essentially, for every college there is a graph where the X-axis is ACT or SAT score and the Y-axis is GPA. Then, it contains information about the number of applicants from your particular high school and which students were *Accepted/Rejected/Wait-listed/*etc. You'll have your own "data point" on each chart so you can easily see where you fall in comparison to other students who graduated from your high school. This will help you determine your likelihood of *Acceptance*.

Students should understand how Naviance works if their high schools participate and if students are also using the Common App, because they need to "match" their Common App and Naviance accounts. This is very easy but pertinent to the whole application process, so it is important that you go slowly enough not to make mistakes. Use these instructions: vimeo.com/73384070.

The Coalition might integrate with Naviance in years to come. For more information, greater detail, and current status of the Coalition, please refer to its website: coalitionforcollegeaccess.org/.

As a new element for the 2016–2017 application season, Cappex introduced a "no-frills" free application to colleges. Its goal is to simplify the college application process by allowing students to apply to a wide range of colleges despite only needing to complete one set of essay questions. Most of the smaller/newer applications (Coalition for Access, Universal Application and Cappex) will not fully link with Naviance for the 2016–2017 application cycle. Although this will certainly affect their ability for widespread usage, this may change in years to come. See cappex.com for more details.

Amanda's Tips for Using Applications

- Allow more time than you think it will take. Applying to college is a long, exhausting process where you must physically type your information again and again, and you want to get it right. Make sure you also leave yourself plenty of time to simply read over your application; my mom has told me a countless number of horror stories about students who realized after it was too late to change inaccurate information.

All my students underestimate this aspect of the process. Nothing about it is hard, but to do it well, it is very time-consuming. Allow double the number of hours you think you will need to type, edit, and edit again.

I have had students call me in a panic after they submitted an application, only to realize that they inputted some data incorrectly. This is 100% avoidable. Please take great care before you submit an application and be sure someone else checks your work.

- Never type your first responses directly into Common App; sometimes the website is funky and will delete your work. I kept a Word document separately for each essay, and I did all of my preliminary work in there. Then, after I checked my spelling for the last time, I copied and pasted into Common App.

Many students think this is not necessary, but then, invariably, they make a mistake and are so thankful that it is not in their Common App. If you print your essay and read it out loud, it is easier to find errors than rereading it electronically. Of course, you will want an English teacher to review it too.

- When it comes to the process of copying and pasting, Common App is very inconsistent. It is essential that you *check* that what you pasted reflects exactly what you copied.

Sometimes you first have to copy and paste into Notes (an application on a Mac), and then copy and paste that into Common App in order for it to work. For me, Common App often truncated my last paragraph of each essay unless I physically copied and pasted the last paragraph by itself. Is it annoying? Yes, absolutely. But it's totally worth it—just don't let the technology mess you up.

Q Every year there seems to be one or more glitches like this on Common App. So again, leave yourself plenty of time and be prepared to get help if you need it.

- Don't get carried away when using programs like Naviance to compare yourself to your peers. I know from experience that it's possible to spend hours on that site and then walk away feeling worse about your prospects. While it's fine to use the application as a comparative tool to get a realistic sense of your college goals, set a timer so you ensure that time does not slip away. You also want to exert caution if you see a small number of applicants with lower GPAs and testing who got admitted to selective colleges. They probably had a hook such as legacy that is not reflected on Naviance scattergrams.

- Keep a record of all your submissions. For example, each time you submit a standardized test score or application and your computer redirects to a "Thank you for submitting" page, screenshot that. You can save all your screenshots to a folder on your desktop to have just in case you need proof. You'll likely never use these, but it's important as a safety net.

- I don't have any personal tips concerning Coalition, Universal, or Cappex because I did not use them. However, I would say that it's important to stay organized, starting in ninth grade, and document everything you might eventually submit to your portfolio. Use folders on your computer to your advantage or use Google Docs—whatever works for you. Making a spreadsheet helps tremendously to identify which types of applications each college on your list accepts.

CHAPTER 15

Interviewing

Colleges that require interviews are part of a dying breed, but these schools are often some of my favorite in the country. It is simply not cost-effective for many colleges to employ admissions counselors who take hours to interview prospective students. However, the colleges that do make interviews a priority truly want to know their applicants on a holistic basis (beyond their statistics).

> **A** I found it refreshing to interview for college because I think that there are so many times when numbers and test scores don't accurately reflect students' abilities. I liked to be able to discuss my interests and curiosities whenever possible. The college process felt more personal through an interview.

These schools want to look beyond the numbers when evaluating students, to assess whether they would fit into the community. Because an interview requires a skill set entirely different from taking an exam in school, admission officers have the opportunity to learn through conversation about their applicants as people. What topics make students' eyes light up and lean forward in their chairs?

A I actually learned in AP Psychology that <u>leaning back in your chair suggests that you are disinterested</u> in what your conversation partner is saying. So, sit up!

Interviews can vary tremendously from one school to another. Some colleges (mostly public institutions) do not offer any form of an interview. Some schools offer interviews with office staff, some with trained students (or a combination), and some offer alumni interviews only.

You should absolutely <u>take advantage of an interview at each school</u> on your list—whether it is required, recommended, or non-evaluative.

A Even when I interviewed with colleges that supposedly granted "non-evaluative" interviews, the interviewers took notes. I think that <u>everything you say counts for something and will help you</u> in the long run.

The first reason is that learning how to conduct yourself favorably in an interview is a lifelong skill you must have for future jobs. Secondly, an interview will not hurt you. Unless you say something completely radical and/or offensive, admission officers who interview you are generally looking to *like* you as an applicant.

Jill's Interview Tips

▶ Eye contact and a firm handshake are really as important as everyone says they are.

▶ Always follow up with a thank-you note. If you can, reference specific topics or pieces of information from your conversation. For example, if you had mentioned that you are very involved in DECA (a high school business club) and the interviewer had never heard of it, you might think about sending him/her a link to an official website when you follow up.

A In one interview I had with a small liberal arts school in Pennsylvania, I mentioned my published article on *Teen Ink*, an online magazine. In my follow-up email, I provided a link to the article. The interviewer apparently took the time to read it because she sent back a few links of articles similar to mine that she thought I would enjoy.

▶ Enter the interview room with three things in mind about yourself that you will definitely say—regardless of the questions asked. If you are nervous about forgetting these topics, it is totally fine to write them down on an index card or piece of paper that you hold during the interview. While you are bound to neglect to mention certain things in any interview, at least you will always have said the three things on your index card.

A My three "things" varied depending on the college. For the most part, I always found a way to mention my participation with Key Club and community service, my love of writing (using my Creative Writing Independent Study and my published work on *Teen Ink* as examples), and my engagement with teachers in high school—showing initiative and my ability to thrive in a small classroom environment and willingness to seek professors outside of the classroom. For colleges with a lot of spirit, I almost always discussed my love of camp and related leadership opportunities that I've had. My enthusiasm for camp (I think) really comes across when I speak about it. Interviewers find it interesting that my best friend lives in Canada; it shows that I can maintain and foster even long-distance relationships and connect with different kinds of people.

▶ Be prepared. It is okay to have another index card listing things to discuss and questions to ask. Prior to the interview, read about your intended major, interests, internships, clubs, and other opportunities that are *specific to that school*.

It is important to show your interviewer that you know a fair amount about the institution and that you are a good "match" for the community. If you know of a special tradition at the college, feel free to mention that as well.

A Mom, this is a little old-school. Despite my mother's warning that it looked unprofessional, I almost always kept my questions on Evernote so I could access the list from my phone or iPad. I never met an interviewer who minded the electronics when used in this fashion.

It's totally worth it to spend time on your research. Usually I prepared for an interview in under a half hour. Keep a list of the clubs that you could "match" to your interests. For example, because I was very involved with my high school newspaper, I always learned the name of the colleges' newspapers and expressed interest in writing for them to my interviewers.

For example, when my Cornell interviewer told me she met her fiancé at Cornell, I asked if she was planning her wedding in Sage Chapel at Cornell where many couples get married. She thought it was cute that I asked. ☺

▶ You can bring a copy of your high school transcript and résumé, but do not give it to your interviewer until the end of your meeting. If you hand it to him/her at the beginning, those documents will suddenly drive the conversation instead of you and your research about the college.

A Most of my interviewers were happy to take my résumé and transcript and put them together with my file. I can imagine that it probably helps them stay organized.

▶ *You* drive the conversation. Do not play defense; play offense. After you answer a question, elaborate on something you mentioned that is important to you. Students who have distinct interests impress admission officers.

Amanda's Interview Tips

- Don't be nervous. Really. The term "interview" is so much more frightening than the experience actually is. An interview with an admissions counselor is simply a conversation during which you talk about your interests and how you would pursue those passions at the particular school.

- You'd be surprised by how much your attitude says about you. Always be friendly and respectful.

- Ask questions. In my experience with interviews, the interviewer *likes* when you are inquisitive because it clearly shows your interest in the school. Prioritize your best questions because the reality is that you may not have time to ask all of them.

CHAPTER 16

Writing Essays and Supplements

Essays might be the most important—yet often most overlooked and underrated—part of your applications. <u>The main essay, or the one you will likely use for multiple colleges through Common App, is often read the least.</u>

> I definitely did not know this until my mom told me. Because I am actually most proud of my Common App essay and think it is one of my best, <u>I was disappointed to learn that</u> from an admissions perspective, it mattered least.

Aside from the fact that this essay is long (<u>650-word limit</u>), admissions personnel know that students use a one-size-fits-all approach because the supplement will fill requirements for many schools.

> Well, relatively long. Six hundred and fifty words is only approximately two typed, double-spaced pages, and you'd be surprised how hard it is to adhere to this word limit. <u>It is very important that you abide by word limit guidelines</u> so that the online application does not truncate your work.

The supplemental essay questions, however, are written by the college admissions staff themselves. They really want to know the answers.

Many colleges ask the question, "Why do you want to come to 'insert school's name here'?"

> **A** I'd say that close to half the colleges on my list either required or recommended that I answer this question about each particular school.

It is crucial that you answer these supplements *very* specifically for each particular school. When you think you have completed the essay, if you could hypothetically plug in the name of another college and still have it make sense, you need to re-write it.

> **A** Don't try to use the same content for multiple "*Why*" supplements because you will never get away with it, especially not if my mom is the editor or reader.

Most things that you mention in your supplement should not even be remotely relatable to more than that one school.

For these "*Why*" supplements, you need to mention the college's specific academic and extracurricular opportunities that interest you. If you were to attend that school, what would you participate in on campus? What classes would you take?

> **A** You should actually take the time to peruse the school's course catalog. For example, for many schools I applied to as an English major, I named specific creative writing classes that I thought sounded interesting.

If you had visited a campus, this is a fantastic time to check your notes and photos to jog your memory.

A For sure. This is when those notes come in handy! I always read through my notes from a college visit before I began that school's "*Why*" supplement. Even looking at pictures you took can help put you in the right mindset to answer the prompt.

You can also peruse the college's website or college guide brochures to learn about special internships, study abroad opportunities, or other interesting programs. Search for the specific names of clubs you might join and name them within your supplement. Remember, no one is going to hold you to what you say—you won't be in trouble if you write about a club in which you end up not participating for whatever reason.

A At first, I had trouble explaining my fascination with a particular school's debate team because I wasn't sure whether the debate team would be a high priority for me in college. However, I genuinely enjoyed my debate experience in high school and was ultimately able to find a way to connect it with something similar at most colleges.

The goal is to demonstrate your grades and activities as a *match* with the college in order to make it an easy decision for admissions officers to admit you. Colleges often use these supplements as a form of Demonstrating Interest because they can tell how much research you have done about their specific programs and opportunities available at no other school (see Chapter 8 on *Demonstrating Interest* and *"Playing the Game"*).

Other supplemental essays are important as well. You may very well be able to use the same essay for multiple colleges if they all ask the same (or similar) questions. A few years ago, I worked with a student who applied to two schools that both asked, "Who would be the person you would most like to have dinner with—dead or alive?" When this happens, it is a no-brainer to submit similar essays. Feel very lucky that you are spared the extra work and absolutely use the same essay twice.

Two colleges on my list had a prompt: "What is the largest problem that confronts the world today?" (or something similar). I was able to tweak only a few sentences and essentially use the essay again.

College admissions officers are creating this type of question mostly to assess your personality and tone when writing, as opposed to your level of match for the school.

 Also, show your creativity. Don't offer a response that is clichéd or ordinary. Part of the fun is crafting your own unique answer.

A supplemental essay is certainly not the place to cut corners on your application. You will need to write a host of essays throughout this process, and if you really want serious consideration, you need to do a good job. All essays and supplements are supposed to be announced by August 1 of each year. (Many colleges miss this deadline, which is irritating since students absolutely need to follow college's deadlines.) If you plan accordingly for the summer before your senior year, you will have time to get a huge jumpstart before high school classes begin.

 I know I'm a little crazy, but I actually completed the bulk of my essays prior to the start of classes. I spent the entire last two weeks of summer sitting at my kitchen table plowing through the essays one at a time. I have to admit that I totally did not realize how much time these supplements would take me. However, I'm glad I dedicated so much energy and thought to them because I really learned a lot about myself in the process. For example, when else do you have the opportunity to respond to open-ended questions about issues such as whether privacy or security is a more important priority? I also discovered what I was looking for more specifically in an ideal college.

Although I have already emphasized the point that the supplemental essays are actually much more important to a college admissions officer than the main essay, I will discuss the main essay briefly because many high school students stress over it. Do not focus on the essay question options or even the story you want to tell. Begin with a brainstorm about interesting moments in your 17 years of life. Your entire essay can be about something that happened over the course of just a few minutes—and often these are very powerful stories.

 Like my essay! The whole scene probably lasted 10 minutes.

It is absolutely essential that your essay have a dramatic opening to catch your reader's attention. Most importantly, you need to convey what you learned about yourself, others, or the world through this essay.

 I thought this was a rather daunting task. Don't think of it like this; just write the essay and have your parents or an English teacher read it. Could they tell that you learned something? However, craft your essay in a way that your character *can* learn something new.

The experience you select needs to have changed you in some way. Many high school students say things to me like, "No one has died or gotten sick in my family, so what will I write about?" The reality, of course, is that those people have much to be thankful for, considering that death and sickness are challenging topics to write about anyway. Even if there *has* been death or sickness within your close circle of family and friends, you may not be emotionally ready to tell that story. Just remember that regardless of what you choose to write about, picture the reader glancing at your essay around 4 o'clock in the afternoon, at the end of a long workday. Perhaps the reader had just had a fight with her fiancé and spilled coffee on her blouse—picture the reader's worst-case scenario. How will that person remember your essay? How will you make your essay stand out, separate from the dozens and hundreds per day that circulate through an admissions office?

> **A** My main essay idea flooded into my semiconscious head one morning at 6 o'clock while I was a counselor at sleep-away camp before senior year. Instead of embarking on my normal morning routine of running the mountain bike trail before my girls woke up, I quickly wrote as much as I possibly could in my notebook. Although the "essay" was very unpolished and my thoughts were jagged and random, I had the idea—and the initial brainstorm was something I had been worrying about for a while. In the end, my essay was about a moment that I experienced with one of my more difficult campers. Through her social struggles of adjusting to camp, demonstrated by a tantrum, I reflected on what camp has meant in my life and how it helped shape the person I am today. I am very proud of the final essay product; <u>it was definitely worth the dozen drafts and hours of time writing and editing.</u> ☺

Your essay writing should be on par with your grades in high school English classes. If you typically get Cs in English and your essay is of "A" quality, the admissions reader will assume you did not write it yourself. Also note that colleges are frequently using programs to check students for plagiarizing. Clearly, your moral integrity is a primary part of this process, so make good decisions and avoid doing anything that could be construed as unethical.

Amanda's Extra Tips for College Essays

- "Plagiarize yourself" whenever possible. For example, seize the opportunity to use the same essay for more than one college's prompt, as long as the questions are not college-specific.
- Never repeat essays for "*Why*" supplements.
- Don't underestimate the number of drafts of each essay you'll need to write before you can be confident about submitting.
- Keep your notes from college visits handy and use them.
- Don't dread writing the essays. While it's a lot of work, it can actually be fun if you treat it like a game: how can you best "match" yourself to each college? My mom always says that students who embrace this aspect of the college process actually end up enjoying it.
- The essays are a part of your application through which colleges can learn qualitative information about you. Don't throw that opportunity away.
- Stay true to your writing "voice." Sound like yourself.

CHAPTER 17

Assessing Types of Applications and Responses

Just like pretty much everything else in this process, admission plans and admission offices' <u>responses are complicated</u>.

> **A** I can barely keep all the different terms straight in my head, even after completing the entire application process! I very much depended upon my chart to organize the various deadlines. Clearly, you don't want to be late for anything, whether it's submitting either a letter of recommendation or a supplemental essay.

There are many deadlines to consider when applying to college and also many ways in which a college can respond to your application—it may not be a simple *Acceptance* or *Rejection*. This chapter will outline more of the common admission plans and decisions.

About 450 colleges offer some type of early admission plan. Depending on the plan, students apply to colleges early and receive a decision early. I have seen firsthand with my students that there is a significant advantage to applying early (at most colleges), compared with your chances if you apply during the "regular" round. Colleges enjoy their early rounds as well because this helps to protect their *Yield*. They know that students who apply early are more likely to attend their institutions if admitted.

There Are Five Types of Admission Plans to Review

1. Rolling Decisions

This plan is frequently offered by the big, state schools, as well as by other schools that basically read applications all year long. Typically, the earlier in the year you apply after August 1 when most applications are released, the better your chances are for getting in. Each university has a certain number of "spots" to offer an incoming class, and these spots fill as the year progresses; it makes sense that applying early gives you an advantage. Depending on the school, you will typically hear from the admissions office anywhere from three to four weeks after your application is complete.

> **A** I was really anxious to submit my applications to Rolling schools as soon as possible. If my mom hadn't needed to check and obsess over every application several times before our submitting them, I probably could have finished earlier (thanks, Mom). In all honesty, though, it was so nice to submit the bulk of my applications by the end of September. I received my first college *Acceptance* in the middle of November.

Imagine how nice it would be to receive an *Acceptance* letter from a college early in your senior year. Keep in mind that according to NACAC, equal consideration is supposed to be granted to *any* application submitted before October 15, so do not panic if you can't get your applications in super early. Because Amanda wanted to participate in the fall musical at school—a very time-consuming activity—she felt as though she needed to have a good jumpstart before school started in order to enjoy being part of the play.

2. Early Decision

Applying <u>Early Decision means signing a *binding contract*</u> with one particular college or university.

> **A** Of course, I am biased, but <u>I love Early Decision</u>. Senior year was much less stressful than it was for most of my friends who had to wait until May or June to decide on their next destinations. While there is no guarantee you'll be admitted Early Decision, throwing your hat in the ring at least gives you a shot—if you're able to commit financially and geographically.

Do not make this decision lightly. You must be absolutely certain that you want to attend this institution if admitted. Early Decision is a big deal and there are several factors to consider before a student and his/her family should participate in the plan:

> ► **Financial.** If you are in a position where you will want/ need to compare financial aid packages among multiple colleges, do not apply Early Decision. My recommendation <u>before applying Early Decision is that you check your EFC</u> (Estimated Family Contribution) at your number one choice college by using its online calculator.

> **A** Understandably, <u>lots of people are money-conscious when considering their college options</u>. Several parents I know told their children that they must go to whatever college gave them the best deal financially, so they clearly could not commit to the Early Decision plan.

> ► **Academic.** There is a huge advantage to applying Early Decision because it is the ultimate form of Demonstrated Interest. Colleges know with certainty that if they offer you admission, you will attend. Clearly, this protects their *Yield*. However, make sure that your grades reflect your academic ability. If you could be doing better, improve your GPA during senior year and then apply to that college in the

regular round or through ED 2 (see the following). There is <u>no advantage to applying Early Decision with poor grades</u>. Applying ED to out-of-reach schools precludes the chance to have applied to a somewhat less selective school where an ED edge may have boosted your chances.

A I know a girl with very low grades and test scores who applied Early Decision to Cornell. She ended up with a *Rejection* letter. The bottom line is that if you have only a "shot in the dark" at a college, maybe it isn't worth the disappointment to apply there Early Decision. Of course, it's a personal decision, but <u>ask for input from your school counselor</u> or teachers about what they think your likelihood is at a particular school. I know my mom always gives her clients "percentages" of what she thinks their chances are at *Acceptance*.

▶ **First choice.** Remember that you can apply Early Decision to only one college because if the institution *Accepts* you with enough financial aid as indicated on your application, you *must* attend. My rule of thumb with my students is that before they apply Early Decision they should have visited 10–12 colleges while they were in session, spent three or four hours on each campus, and <u>revisited the Early Decision contender a second or a third time</u>. I realize that this sounds extreme—and expensive. If you can visit only seven or eight colleges, that is fine too. Just remember that you must be ready to make an absolute commitment if applying Early Decision.

A The requirement to visit 10–12 colleges was easy for me, given my mom's job. By senior year I had been to well over 50 colleges. I had already visited Cornell multiple times over the years, but <u>I went back in August of senior year</u> just to make sure that it was my absolute first choice.

I had spent April break of my junior year revisiting the five schools I was considering for Early Decision.

▶ **Early Decision 1 and 2.** A more recent trend is for colleges to offer both Early Decision 1 and Early Decision 2 deadlines. The Early Decision 2 deadline gives you about a month's more time to decide on your first choice, but both Early Decision 1 and Early Decision 2 have the same rules regarding the binding contract. Many students apply Early Decision 2 to a college after being *Rejected* or *Deferred* from their Early Decision 1 schools.

> **A** I briefly considered applying Early Decision 2 somewhere if I had been *Rejected* from Cornell. However, I decided that I did not want to tie myself to any one school if *Denied* from my first choice—I wanted the ability to weigh my other options. And, several of my other top contenders did not offer the ED 2 option. The people in my school who applied Early Decision 2 were *Accepted* sometime in February. Some of these students had earlier been *Rejected* from top-tier schools in the Early Decision 1 round, and a few of them just applied Early Decision 2 because they needed a little more time to narrow down their options. Also keep in mind that not all schools offer Early Decision 2, even if they have Early Decision 1.

However, keep in mind that colleges are aware of this trick, as are thousands of students—the Early Decision 2 applicant pool can be very competitive because it is comprised of several "Ivy rejects." ED 2 is a relatively new option, but it is increasing in popularity as another option for colleges to secure their classes. Many colleges are filling more than 50% of their class through ED applicants!

▶ **Other options.** You can (and absolutely should) apply to other colleges if you decide to seek *Acceptance* to any college Early Decision.

> **A** Definitely. The security of knowing I was *Accepted* to great schools even before I heard from Cornell dramatically lessened the stress of the entire process.

Remember, though, that you must withdraw all other applications if you are *Accepted* Early Decision to allow the college to fill your space. It is only fair to do this for your peers and for the colleges, which are anxious to fill their spots. However, make sure you don't have "all your eggs in one basket" by refusing to apply to other schools.

A Two days after the Thursday night I was *Accepted* to Cornell, I emailed all the admissions representatives for other schools to inform them that I would not be attending their institutions. Several friends that got in Early Decision were not quite so quick to inform other colleges of their decisions, which is fine too. As long as you notify them way before the deadline for regular applicant submissions, you are being respectful of students really hoping to be admitted to these schools. However, it probably works to your advantage to let these schools know as soon as possible because then you'll stop receiving promotional advertisements at your home and email addresses. It's nice to commit to one school and no longer be bombarded by both the College Board and the colleges themselves!

I require my private clients to apply to at least six other colleges before they hear from their ED schools. I do this for two important reasons. First of all, not getting in ED is a huge disappointment. Not getting in and then having to start the application process is worse. Your head is not "in it," making it difficult to put your best foot forward. Secondly, many colleges use the date of your early application submission as a form of Demonstrating Interest.

3. Early Action

You are able to apply to as many colleges as you would like with an Early Action plan. If you are *Accepted* to one particular college, you can either commit immediately or wait until the spring to decide, once you have assessed your other options. You can also decline the offer at any time. I personally love Early Action because you can apply early and hear early without the pressure of the binding commitment inherent in Early Decision.

> I like it too. I applied to several schools with the Early Action plan. If a school had that option, I took advantage of it. Why not? It's a great way to Demonstrate Interest and receive a response early.

4. Single-Choice Early Action (SCEA)

This relatively new option offered by a select group of colleges may seem a bit confusing at first. Students are only allowed to apply SCEA to one college. If a student applies SCEA, he/she is not allowed to apply Early Decision or Early Action to any other college. If *Rejected* under SCEA process, a student may apply Regular Decision or Rolling Decision to other schools. Additionally, some schools stipulate under SCEA that you may apply to another college's Early Decision 2, but you can only do so if the notification of admission occurs after January 1. In this case, if you were admitted through another college's Early Decision 2 program, you would have to withdraw your SCEA application!

> None of my friends did this, but it sounds like a good option if you don't want to commit to Early Decision 1. Cornell only had ED 1 with a November deadline.

5. Restrictive Early Action (REA)

This is a non-binding option. Students are only allowed to apply REA to one college. Students who apply through REA cannot simultaneously apply Early Decision. However, students who apply REA may still apply Early Action to other schools.

While I know that the nitty-gritty rules are hard to follow, try not to worry. Determine to which colleges you are applying and then look at each school's options individually. Every college or university has very specific guidelines on its website, and you can also call a school and ask an admissions counselor.

A Also, I'm telling you: <u>use a chart or Excel spreadsheet to orga-nize your deadlines</u>—it's so easy and helpful for quick fact-checking.

Regardless of which way you apply to a school be sure to keep your school counselor in the loop well ahead of deadlines, to guarantee you understand the rules. Your school counselor also needs to submit your transcript and Letter of Recommendation on time, so <u>it is important that he/she is aware of submission deadlines</u> for applicant materials.

A My high school guidance department requires seniors to fill out a chart of all the schools to which we applied and to list each school's deadline. Even if your school counselor does not officially request this type of record, <u>it can't hurt to remind him/her of your important deadlines</u>.

• • •

The next portion of this chapter examines the types of responses from colleges. It is important to read the "fine print" when you get a letter or email bearing your admissions decision. Sometimes, it can be an *"Admit"* or a *"Deny,"* which is clearly straightforward. However, there are an increasing number of ways for colleges to admit students under certain special "terms." Two common types of these responses are *Waitlist* and *Deferral*. A much less common response, but one that is appearing with increasing frequency, is the *Guaranteed Transfer*. With these cases, if possible, <u>I suggest that students "move on" emotionally</u> from the school, and psychologi-cally consider it almost a *Rejection*.

A Mom, most people don't do this if their hearts are set on a particular school. Knowing that there's still <u>a small chance of Acceptance probably makes it pretty hard to outright withdraw your application</u>.

While the college is pursuing other students, you may want to pursue other colleges. Although some colleges *Accept* students from a *Waitlist* or after *Deferral*, students should not count on this. Hopefully, all students have college lists that include *only* schools that they love—pick another one.

> I know many more people who were *Rejected* after a *Deferral* than people who were *Accepted*, unfortunately. My friends on *Waitlists* usually chose other schools because waiting until June or July to decide where you're going is super stressful.

Waitlist (WL)

A *Waitlist* technically means that the college would like to *Accept* you, but does not currently have room in its freshman class for you, given the number of students it already *Accepted*.

> This was the case for a few of my friends. While they were qualified in terms of academics and extracurriculars for top-tier schools, they were *Waitlisted* at a bunch. Too bad they had not applied Early Decision because by demonstrating their interest early, they may have had a better shot.

Another possibility is that the college does not want to *Accept* you, but it also does not want to upset you or your parents because of a Legacy/Donor relationship.

> One person I knew had legacy at a great liberal arts school. He applied Early Decision but got *Deferred* and then *Waitlisted* in the regular round. There was a lot of uncertainty for months, but he eventually was taken off the *Waitlist* and is now enrolled at that school—it had always been his first choice.

Instead of *Rejecting* you, a school can "soften the blow" with a *Waitlist* decision. This is being used more widely in recent years and substantially helps colleges, not students. Getting off a WL from the most selective schools is very difficult.

Perhaps the biggest issue with *Waitlist* is that it can make senior year feel like an emotional roller coaster. Your likelihood of getting removed from a *Waitlist* varies significantly from one school to another and even from one year to the next. A lot will depend on how well a particular admissions team did the previous year in terms of enrollment and filling all possible spaces. Another way to think about the job of an admissions department is that it needs to fill all the school's beds with qualified applicants from diverse geographical, technological, social, and religious backgrounds. This is a tall order.

A As hard as it is for us seniors actually applying to college, think about how difficult it must be to narrow down such a large pool of qualified applicants while trying to maintain as much diversification as possible.

When a student receives a *Waitlist* decision, the situation can become very emotional. For starters, colleges rarely notify students before May 1 about whether they are taken off *Waitlists*, and therefore students usually send a deposit somewhere else first to secure a position.

A Several people in my grade wanted to hold out for a *Waitlist* at certain colleges and did not hear their decisions until the middle of July. Most of them deposited tuition somewhere else, but it was hard to have to wait so long to find out.

Also, *Waitlists* prolong the already lengthy college process and make families and students feel unsettled about the future. Students are not allowed to "double deposit" by sending deposits to two universities and thinking about them after May 1. However, sending in a deposit while keeping a place on a *Waitlist* is okay because even after doing so you are not technically *Accepted* to the school that gave you the WL response.

Waitlists help colleges a lot more than they do students. Remember that the single most important factor to colleges is protecting their *Yield* (see Chapter 8 on *Demonstrating Interest and "Playing the Game"*), and a *Waitlist* assists colleges in doing just that. *Waitlists* are becoming a more common trend, especially among top-tier colleges that may stipulate a scenario like this: a college will place students on a *Waitlist*. Then, in the middle of the summer, the college representatives call the students to say something like, "*IF* we take you off our *Waitlist*, will you definitely attend our institution? You have 24 hours to decide." If you say that you will 100% commit, this institution will send you an *Acceptance* letter.

 Yikes! Talk about pressure.

While none of my clients have ever received this phone call, I know of numerous students who have.

 I only know of one. It must have been crazy for him—he was super close to attending four different schools at different points after May 1.

If you have been reading this book thoroughly, you know by now that this is all a trick for the college to protect its *Yield*: if the student declines this phone call offer, he/she was never technically *Accepted* by the college and therefore does not negatively impact the college's *Yield*.

 Tricky, tricky. This is smart on the part of colleges, but they need to have some sympathy for high schoolers.

Conversely, if the student *Accepts*, the college's *Yield* is augmented because the school is guaranteed to receive enrollment from the student. Personally, as a college counselor and advocate for children, this is frustrating. While ultimately students could be excited (which is great), I do not like anything that helps only colleges and not students. The good news is that this does not happen often because most colleges try to finish with the WL by early July.

Deferral

A *Deferral* is a college's response to an Early Action or Early Decision applicant and is also growing in popularity as a way to help colleges, not necessarily students. There are two common possible reasons for *Deferral*. Sometimes it means that the school wants to wait to compare you to regular applicants in a few months and have another look at your application.

 Nearly all my friends were *Deferred* from at least one school… and so was I.

However, particularly with huge state schools, a *Deferral* may mean that though you submitted your application in time for an *Early* deadline, the college was so inundated with early applications that admissions counselors simply did not yet have time to read your application. The latter is so frustrating. Students do their work to submit their applications promptly, yet some colleges must *Defer* them to the regular round because the schools simply run out of time.

 I know for a fact that one popular state school *Defers* students for this reason very often. When one of my qualified friends was *Deferred* and called to ask why, the admissions officer told her that no one had glanced at her application yet. I guess it depends on where your application falls in the "pile," which is one incentive to get your submissions done as soon as possible. These state schools get so busy that you need to submit your application as soon as it's ready.

In many cases, a *Deferral* is probably a nice manner of *Rejection*. If given a particularly high number of applications to review in the regular round, colleges do not always have the time to go back to review the early applications—unless there is new information presented like better grades in the three months between the two decision rounds (more on this later in the chapter).

> **A** Mom, you also wanted me to reach out to my admissions officers at key points throughout the college process. As much as I complained prior to sending these emails, I think it may have improved my chances at my *Likely Schools* and *Target Schools* by Demonstrating Interest.

My general advice to students who are *Wait-listed* or *Deferred* is to psychologically move on if possible. If the school was your top choice and you were not *Accepted* to your other top contender colleges, perhaps you would decide to stay on the list. Regardless, it is a tough decision. If, however, you opt to stay on a *Waitlist*, here are a few pieces of advice for senior year to assist in maximizing your admission chances and understanding the likelihood of *Acceptance*:

> **A** I don't know of too many people in my school who actually did any of these things. Maybe they could have helped themselves get removed from the *Waitlists*. This is good advice, even if it requires some extra work and planning.

- ▶ Look up the college's statistics from the last three years to gauge a sense of how many students were taken off the *Waitlist*. Remember that this number will likely vary from year to year.
- ▶ You should send the college an email notifying the admissions office of your intention to stay on the *Waitlist* and that you will *Attend* if you are *Admitted*. It is important to say this—but only if it is true, as colleges want to protect their *Yield* and are more likely to *Accept* you. While it is

important to Demonstrate Interest in this way, my advice is that you wait until after the New Year and then email or even call or visit if you can. Many students who have been *Deferred* and *Waitlisted* call colleges as soon as they have released the results from their early rounds, and admissions offices are often very hectic at this time. The admissions staff needs a holiday too.

▶ A *Waitlisted* student should <u>think of the experience like a campaign</u>: it takes perseverance. Always keep in mind that admissions officers are focused on their *Yield*, so when it comes time to admit students from the *Waitlist*, they will select the students who they think are most likely to enroll.

A Distinguish yourself from other students in similar positions by <u>personally contacting admissions officers</u>. My experience is that, especially for smaller, liberal arts schools, the admission counselors are very happy to hear from prospective students. They do not find emails annoying if written sparingly and tastefully.

▶ If you have won any awards or <u>anything substantial has happened to you</u> since you first sent in your application (such as winning a science or music competition), this is a great time to tell the school.

A I remember that we debated about whether to inform colleges of my straight As for the first quarter of senior year. We eventually decided that the tone was too "braggy." However, <u>if there is a particular class in which you excelled</u> and that maybe stands out from your typical academic performance, perhaps you would tell the schools about your grades.

In this email, you should explain your rationale for applying to that particular school, why you are a good fit, and what makes the school a top choice for you. Be as specific as possible and use colorful details that aid in linking your high school experiences to goals in your future. If possible, inform the college of why attending that institution would help you meet your academic and educational goals, and mention specifically what programs you would participate in if *Admitted*. You can treat the email like a "*Why*" supplement.

▶ Ideally, you should visit the campus again and personally meet with someone in admissions. I know it is expensive to travel, but if you are really committed to one college and want to spend the next four years there more than anything, showing up and telling the office is a good idea if you are on the border of a *Waitlist*. Your visit signals to the college that you are serious about attending the institution.

▶ Sending a few additional letters of recommendation at this time could also help dramatically. You never know if just one teacher's powerful words can push your application over the edge. Recommendations must be written by people who know you well and can attest to both your qualities and the reasons for your "match" to the college. If possible, recommenders should be aware that the people reading these letters are knee-deep in applications at this point and have not slept well in weeks. In order to be effective, the letters need to be written in a way that catches the reader's attention and the specific college's mission and culture.

▶ If you are able to make another visit to the school, arrange for an interview. Connecting with admissions officers can only help at this point.

Guaranteed Transfer

Although less common than *Deferrals* and *Waitlists*, an increasing trend for colleges is the *Guaranteed Transfer*. Schools define this term in multiple ways, but typically this offer includes an opportunity to transfer to that particular college at the onset of sophomore year.

A Cornell's common plan is the Guaranteed Spring Transfer, where a student is required to attend another institution for the first semester and then can join Cornell for the second semester. I know a few people who were offered this plan of admission.

The stipulations can vary greatly, but typically students are supposed to attend another accredited institution for one year beforehand. They must remain in good academic and disciplinary standing, and they need to file forms before the transfer occurs for their second year.

Some schools will *Accept* students with the condition that they must first study abroad or at another institution for a semester or a year, depending on the college's demands. Admissions offices often use these programs to secure weak students and/or prospective students with legacy. Instead of outright *Rejecting* students, the college will offer them a spot—with several strings attached. Very often, students and their families do not like this route because it's a non-traditional way to attend college. However, I have seen plenty of students make these offers work for their situations after they weigh their options.

A One of my older friends was able to attend a great city college after completing a semester abroad during freshman year and taking classes for college credit.

These students end up exploring or pursuing other interests—perhaps taking a gap year or studying in another academic field—and are still able to attend the college of their choice eventually. As a plea to school counselors, given all the flexibility that colleges allow themselves about informing students of their decisions past May 1, I ask you to consider having "College Day" in your high schools (when students typically wear their college's logo clothing) on June 1 or the last day of classes. Calendars vary throughout the nation, but many seniors do not yet know on May 1 where they will be in the fall. It makes me sad that they cannot enjoy College Day like most of their friends.

With regard to taking a gap year, I think it is an amazing opportunity for students. It will not enhance your chances of admission, since you apply to college as a senior and then ask a particular school to which you have been *Accepted* for permission to take a gap year. However, it is the gift of time: time to grow up and time to take a breath as you think about the next chapter of life with a little more clarity. Gap years used to be considered a waste of time. Now, so many colleges (including the Ivies and top-tiers) fully support a gap year and welcome the opportunity for their students. In fact, Harvard offers all admitted incoming freshman the option of taking a gap year. According to the Center for Interim Programs' "2016 Facts and Figures," Colorado College has an annual goal to have 20% of its incoming freshman class take a gap year. According to Mark Hatch, VP of Enrollment at Colorado College, students who take a gap year have higher GPAs in college than their non-gap year peers, take less time to graduate, and tend to be leaders on campus. Perhaps you are getting burnt out and need a break. This should not be a year off but rather a year to regroup. The year should be organized and a constructive use of time. Volunteering, traveling, and working are all solid options. Mechanically, it is better to apply to college during senior year as you planned. Then, once you are *Accepted*, you can ask to *Defer* the offer and take a year off. A college can deny your request, but my experience is that most colleges want to encourage their students to take the time they need, enabling them to start college with renewed focus, energy and maturity.

Here are a few resources if you want to consider taking a year off before attending college:

dynamy.org
studyoverseas.com
gapyear.com
seamester.com
semesteratsea.org
nationalservice.gov/programs/americorps
iicd-volunteer.org
camphill.org
nascc.org
globalservicecorps.org
nols.edu
outwardbound.org
wheretherebedragons.com
youngjudaea.org

CHAPTER 18

Procuring Financial Aid

You should know upfront that while I am a college expert, I am by no means a financial aid authority. This chapter will provide an overview of financial aid and some tips to use throughout the process, but please consult with an accountant or financial planner to help you manage the cost of college. Many of my tips are actually sourced from experts, and are noted as such below.

I always tell my students' parents that they are "allowed" to pay (or not pay) for all of college, some of college, or none of college. However, by the spring of a child's junior year in high school, the parents must make their financial intentions very clear to their children. When I was a school guidance counselor years ago, I had a student who set his heart on one particular top-tier college—for all the right reasons. He had a sterling transcript, high standardized-test scores, stellar extracurricular activities, had visited the campus, and matched the personality and culture of the university. However, after he was *Accepted* to the school of his dreams, his parents informed him that he could not attend because they were unable to afford the four-year tuition. They had never given him any financial limitations, nor had he been restricted from applying to particular schools. I have no problem with academically strong students applying to expensive colleges, so long as their parents (or whoever is paying for college) make it clear exactly what will happen if they do not receive a specific amount of merit money or financial aid from the college. This conversation should happen *before* the student chooses to do work necessary to complete a school's application. It is unfair if the student is uninformed of financial limitations prior to applying. In the case I just referenced, the parents had thought to themselves, "He'll never get in, so he can just apply." However, he *did* gain admission and, because he badly wanted to attend, understandably felt miserable when his parents said no. This is a disastrous situation, but is totally avoidable if handled correctly from the outset. For example, by using a college's online Net Price Calculator, families can determine how their finances will be used at any school.

After that experience, I have always told the moms and dads that they must determine if they have *any* limitations for their child's college decision. Perhaps the parents can only afford (or only want) to spend a certain amount on college tuition. Maybe they want their child to attend a school that is a certain distance or number of hours away from home. These are normal concerns and definitely "allowed"—parents simply need to share their limitations with their child before the list gets finalized or the child sends any applications. The spring semester of junior year is typically a good time to engage in this important discussion.

The term *financial aid* can be confusing. In general, it refers to any money that you receive to help pay for college—but not all packages are equal. For example, a work-study program is a nice opportunity to get a reasonably enjoyable job on campus while earning some money for school. A loan is money lent to you that you are expected to pay back eventually. On the other hand, grants and scholarships do not need to be paid back.

The next part of this chapter contains a list of terms related to financial aid. I encourage families to review these definitions before the students begin applying to college.

Cost of attendance. This is simply the "sticker price" at a particular college. Cost of attendance includes all expenses such as tuition, extra fees, room, board, textbooks, school supplies, a meal plan, and other living expenses such as transportation. Most students do not pay a college's sticker price. I should mention that *if* you are in a financial position that you can afford and are willing to pay for the entire cost of college attendance, this might be considered a "hook" to some colleges that consider financial need in the admissions process.

Demonstrated need. This is the difference between your expected family contribution (EFC—see the following) and the total cost of attendance.

Expected family contribution. This is a financial aid formula that estimates how much of a college's sticker price you can afford to pay based on factors such as parent income, assets, and family size. EFC can vary considerably for each college.

Gapping. A financial aid gap occurs when a college's financial aid award does not meet the student's financial need. Gapping is a big concern because the student will be responsible for the unmet need in addition to the EFC. You can check the IPEDs website (nces.ed.gov/ipeds) to learn how much each college meets designated need.

Grants. Money that you are not obligated to pay back. Grants are usually assigned based on your family's financial need.

Merit aid/Non-need-based aid. These are two terms to describe money awarded to students without regard to financial need. Merit aid can be received based on academic achievement, artistic ability, leadership skills, or anything else that distinguished you in high school. This has actually become a way for some colleges to lure stronger students by making the cost of college financially appealing.

Need-aware admission. This helps colleges identify which prospective students can afford to pay for college. It is a growing trend, as some colleges consider ability to pay when *Admitting* or *Rejecting* applicants. Few colleges are completely need-blind (see the following).

Need-based aid. This is money awarded to students whose families cannot afford to pay the full price of college. This type of aid may come in different forms; typically, aid comes from grants or scholarships, but sometimes it comes from loans with lower interest rates.

Need-blind admission. A unique (and infrequent) process by which colleges *Accept* students without regard to their financial needs. Unless a college is extremely well-endowed financially and generous with its aid money, however, need-blind admission can mean that a student may be *Accepted* but then not have enough money to actually attend. Some of the wealthiest colleges are now need-blind (other than with development cases) and can afford to meet the demonstrated need of applicants' families.

Net price. This is the amount that you will actually pay for college after tuition discounts, scholarships, and grants are factored into the package. The net price for private colleges is usually substantially less than the sticker price.

Perkins Loan. This is a federal loan for low-income students. With interest rates that are relatively minimal, Perkins Loans also give applicants more time to submit their first payments than other loan programs provide.

Scholarship. This is simply money that applicants do not have to pay back. Scholarships are usually determined as a result of specific applicant qualities and can be categorized as either merit-based or need-based. Whole institutions, as well as individual departments, offer scholarships, as do thousands of nonprofit groups, businesses, and other organizations. While it is admirable to apply for as many scholarships as you can, scholarships often require a lot of work to procure a relatively small amount of money. The best avenue to receive the most "easy money" (scholarships that do not require a lot of extra work) is applying to well-endowed, financially generous colleges whose average students have lower standardized test scores and grade point averages than you do. Colleges want strong students and will sometimes pay to help lure these superstars to attend their institutions. Many schools fall into this category.

There are so many scholarship websites. For the most part, you should not have to pay money to get money, but there are a few exceptions. I have listed below several websites that you may find useful for exploring scholarship opportunities. Talking to your school counselor is a great first step because they are often privy to some good information. If you want to try to research on your own, here are some places to start:

- Cappex.com—Centralized and comprehensive website dedicated to matching students with merit-based scholarships from colleges across the country.
- Collegescholarships.org—Free website that takes you straight to the scholarships that interest you. All the scholarships are easy and simple to view. There is also advice on applying for scholarships.
- Fastweb.com—Free resource for paying and preparing for college. It is committed to providing a quality scholarship matching service, while at the same time protecting its members.
- ScholarshipExperts.com—Free way to find scholarships on the Internet. It delivers accurate and timely search results that have been filtered and customized.
- Scholarships.com—Free scholarship search service and financial aid information resource.

- Schoolsoup.com—Website provides students with the most scholarship and other financial aid on the Internet. Also has a matching platform.
- Studentscholarshipsearch.com—Search, investigate, and apply for scholarships. The website has a scholarship match feature and offers tips and advice, as well.
- MyScholly.com (There is a fee for this one)
- tuitionfundingsources.com
- scholarshippoints.com
- findtuition.com
- unigo.com
- CollegeAnswer.com/scholarships
- chegg.com/scholarships
- petersons.com

Subsidized Stafford Loans. These are federal loans specifically for undergraduate students, and are also known as *direct subsidized loans*. They have slightly better terms than the unsubsidized loans (see below). Subsidized loans are awarded based on financial need. Interest does not start accruing until you enter repayment after leaving college.

Unsubsidized Stafford Loans. These are also federal loans, but are available to both undergraduate and graduate students. There is no financial need requirement, so any applicant can qualify for these loans. Interest rates can vary. In the last few years, the rates have been equal to subsidized loans. However, interest on unsubsidized loans starts adding up from the day you take out the loan.

Work-study. This is a program in which college students are given jobs on campus to help defray their education costs. While there is a large Federal Work-Study program that many colleges offer, some colleges have their own programs as well.

As of 2016, students will fill out college applications and the Free Application for Federal Student Aid (FAFSA) at the same time. The new FAFSA filing date is October 1 of senior year. While this creates an extra busy September for students, FAFSA's intention is to give families more time to learn about their financial circumstances and plan ahead for college. FAFSA will collect income information from the tax/calendar year one year earlier than it has collected these records in the past. This is called Prior-Prior Year (PPY) Tax Year. The only problem with PPY is that it means families must fill out more forms earlier in the year, which can add to the already overwhelming process. I do think families will ultimately embrace knowing their financial realities with college earlier in the process, and I am glad to see the change. Ideally, your family has a trusted accountant or financial planner who can ease stress of financial forms and help your child receive the most aid possible given the circumstances. If you cannot afford an accountant, most financial aid officers (even local ones at institutions to which you may not be applying) are generous with their time. When people have questions about financial forms, they are able to answer most general questions knowledgeably, so don't be afraid to make a few phone calls.

Here are several tips for families to minimize mistakes:

- Remember that the first "F" in FAFSA stands for *FREE*. This means that you should *not* pay to complete forms. Any website asking you for money to apply for free aid is likely a scam.
- The official website is fafsa.ed.gov/. It is a good idea to become familiar with FAFSA's terms well before it is time to apply for college.
- The first financial step that students and parents must take is to get a FSA ID, which includes a username and password. Keep in mind that this process may take a few days

before you are able to access your account. Another reason to do this as early as possible is that financial aid is given out on a first come, first served basis. If you submit your forms early and accurately, you will hold a spot at the front of the line for aid. Priority filing dates vary significantly by college, so you will need to check with individual financial aid offices to get their specific deadlines.

▶ It is more than okay to provide only an estimated tax number on your forms so that you do not miss any deadlines.

▶ Very often, parents complete the FAFSA on behalf of their children. This is fine, but it is technically the student's application. When the FAFSA says *you*, it is referring to the student. If the question is asking about the parent, the form will specify this.

▶ If parents are divorced or separated, steps need to be taken to ensure that the correct person completes the form. The parent responsible for the FAFSA should be the one in whose home the student resides for more than half the year.

▶ Do not use any nicknames when completing any FAFSA documents (or on any official documents).

▶ A common mistake is to leave questions blank. If a particular question does not apply to you for whatever reason, write in a "0." If you leave a question completely blank, the processor will assume you forgot to answer the question; too many blank spaces could cause a miscalculation or rejection.

▶ It is fine to round numbers to the nearest dollar.

▶ It sounds silly, but you must remember to check and recheck that you entered the correct social security number and date of birth. No aid will be awarded until all numbers match with those the federal government already has in its system.

- Do not forget to sign your form. If you are filing the form electronically, use your FSA ID. Without a signature, the form is considered incomplete.
- Count yourself (the student) as a member of the household. The FAFSA includes a specific definition of how to measure your parents' household income, so follow those directions carefully. Additionally, even though a prior conviction does not necessarily disqualify you from federal aid, you should call the Information Center 1-800-433-3243 before leaving blank a question about drug-related offenses.
- Income tax is *not* the same as income. You need to use the 1040 federal tax return for income and reporting paid taxes. Do not use your W-2. If you are a male between the ages of 18 and 26 and fail to register with Selective Service, you will be ineligible for federal student aid.
- You should list on the FAFSA all institutions you are considering. Colleges can no longer see all the schools on the FAFSA, so it will expedite and not harm the application process if you include all potential colleges.
- Many private colleges also require a CSS Profile, Institutional, and/or Verification Form in addition to the FAFSA. There are a lot of overlaps among these extra forms and the FAFSA, but you must be sure to answer all questions consistently; failure to do so could result in lost aid. Extra forms are filed separately from the FAFSA, but please keep copies of everything.

▶ Fill out all forms to the best of your ability, and seek help to ensure that you are completing them accurately. I think it goes without saying that deliberately providing incorrect information to the federal government is a huge mistake, and may result in severe consequences. To ensure that your FAFSA is complete, you can check its status immediately after you submit online.

If you are thinking about whether to apply, you should know that almost everyone qualifies for a federal loan. Unfortunately, your life could at any point take an unexpected turn that suddenly places you in a financial crisis. It is much better to have a completed FAFSA on file in case there is an emergency and your financial situation changes.

I received some of the information included in this chapter from the following resources:

▶ fafsa.ed.gov

▶ "15 Financial Aid Terms Every College Student (and Parent) Should Know," Kaitlin Mulhere, *Time.com*, Jan. 15, 2016

▶ "FAFSA mistakes you can and should avoid," Nancy Griesemer, launchphase2.com/fafsa-mistakes-you-can-and-should-avoid. Feb. 21, 2016

Amanda's Financial Planning Tips

While I definitely won't pretend to have expertise in anything related to applying for Financial Aid, I can offer my thoughts about making and saving money in high school.

- It is not at all difficult to find part-time employment while in high school. Especially during senior year when less of your time is consumed by homework (after you finish applying to college), you certainly could get a job. Many of my friends worked as waitresses or ice cream scoopers during our last year in high school. Although many places pay 18-year-olds only minimum wage, something is better than nothing.

- I personally love working with kids. Starting work as a babysitter in eighth grade, I was able to develop really nice relationships with a few local families who trust me. I love the perks of babysitting: you can always say "no" if you have something else to do; you get to play with cute kids; and after they go to sleep, the time is yours to study or watch TV or whatever.

- When I had more time during the last few months of senior year, I also began tutoring. I absolutely loved it. I genuinely enjoyed explaining fourth grade math concepts and working with a first-grader to get him to sit still and focus for 15 minutes to complete two worksheets.

- One of my friends got a job at a rock climbing gym in a nearby town. She made so many friends by working with other kids about the same age, and enjoyed the sense of community it provided her.

- Another friend worked as a receptionist at a yoga studio, and instead of receiving money for her work, she received free gym classes.

- Yet another worked as a cashier in a supermarket and said she actually enjoyed the routine motions and schedule of working and ringing up customer items.

- Regardless of your job preference, believe me, it feels really good to earn money. Even if you do not spend it all right away (and you probably shouldn't, although I'm no financial advisor), it is nice to save and give. You will want extra spending money when you get to college; even if your parents supply you with some, it can't hurt to have more.

PART III

MENTAL HEALTH

CHAPTER 19

Maintaining Positivity and Optimism

Honestly, I used to have the "Are you kidding me?" attitude when people told me to stay positive about the college process. I thought optimism was overrated, and how much could it really contribute to results anyway? However, as a result of meeting and interacting with different kinds of people through my hometown, summer camp, and clubs and activities such as Key Club, I've learned that your attitude toward any particular project can really determine your success. For example, I remember that when I was a little girl in camp my friends all dreaded soccer or basketball. Their pessimism brought down the excitement of the whole group and set the mood for the rest of the day.

Optimism works in exactly the opposite way. I really believe that if you have a good attitude and believe in your ability, you will do better than you would have if you had never considered your capabilities. It's so easy to lose a positive perspective throughout this process, especially when you get your first *Rejection*. If you have a mantra to repeat, though, you'll begin to believe that the mantra is true—and then that will become reality. As ordinary as it sounds, I personally respond well to the sentence, "I got this." I repeated it over and over at any point when I needed some strength and motivation. For example, I said it before each section of the

ACT, when I had to buckle down and study for a classroom test, and even when I was auditioning for a play as an extracurricular activity and wanted a part. These three simple words gave me a surge of control and adrenaline along with power and composure, and I was able to push through regardless of what the task entailed.

> *I* This did not come easily for you, Amanda. As a little girl, you definitely struggled with the concept, but as you have worked on it you have become so good at <u>positive self-talk</u>. I am so proud!

Here are some other mantras I find helpful:
- ▶ "I'm ready."
- ▶ "I can do this."
- ▶ "I'm as prepared as I'll ever be."
- ▶ "Knock this one out of the park."

I've also found that it helps when you insert your name into these sentences. Don't worry—no one will know you're talking to yourself if you say it in your head. ☺ Addressing yourself will make you more responsible for your actions. Just as you probably listen more intently to anyone if he/she begins the sentence with your name or title, your brain will likely snap to attention when you firmly address the person to whom you are talking (in this case, yourself).

Positive self-talk is a legitimate thing—I did not just make it up. One friend comes to mind immediately when I consider how deeply your words can influence your performance. She is the queen of negative energy. Even a few minutes before a test, she says things like, "I'm going to fail" and "I don't know anything." Regardless of whether these statements are true—and if you studied at all, they're probably not—there is absolutely no good that can result from talking like that. When you look at yourself in the mirror, be kind to yourself and only say things that will propel you through the task at hand. I cannot think of any scenario in which telling yourself that you'll fail would be beneficial for your psyche.

I learned in AP Psychology that "power posing" can also be a helpful influence on your performance on a particular task at hand. There are TED talks and professional studies about power posing, but essentially it involves making your body take up as much space as possible: extend your arms; spread your legs; do something crazy. While you are in this pose, repeat your mantra. As a result, you will feel more powerful.

 I think yoga works really well, also. When I need to shake things up, I will often stand on my head. Reversing my blood flow gives me a new perspective, both literally and figuratively.

There are also other techniques that I have read and learned about through the years. One works when you doubt yourself at any moment during a test. For example, let's say you come to an especially difficult math problem on the ACT. You can design a "reset motion" such as tapping your knee with your pencil three times or patting your head. If you practice this motion often enough prior to the stress-inducing experience, you are supposed to respond to it during the actual situation by being able to take a deep breath and essentially "reset" your thought process. While I did not use a motion, I liked the concept of resetting my brain when I was stuck. If I attacked the problem from a different angle or simply decided to come back to it in a few minutes, I often met with more success.

I know it sounds terribly clichéd, but if you convince yourself that you can do something, you probably can. It drives me crazy when my friends don't realize this and continue to produce negative energy. Don't convince yourself that a test will be hard or impossible, because if you do you'll have a much harder time conquering the exam. Once you find your mantra, you'll be able to do anything you say.

Amen!

CHAPTER 20

Keeping Your Mouth Shut!

To some, this concept will come very easily. If you've grown up with the mindset that sharing grades and scores is distasteful, you can skip this chapter because you already committed to the advice that follows.

However, if you attend a high school in which everyone is involved in everyone else's business about grades and test scores, it might be more difficult. Take it from a girl from a super-competitive public school: <u>avoiding invasive questions gets more difficult</u> the closer you get to the college process and decision releases.

And having worked with students from all types of high schools, I can tell you that I recommend the <u>"keep your mouth shut"</u> philosophy to all my students.

I have been blessed with having a mom who is a college counselor and therefore definitely more knowledgeable than my friends' parents are about all things college. However, contrary to public opinion, I haven't had this whole thing figured out since birth. My <u>mom did not have a preconceived college plan for me.</u>

> *It may sound trite, but I genuinely wanted Amanda to take her own journey to college. As her mom, I wanted to be there to support and guide her, but Amanda was most definitely in the driver's seat.*

As early as when I attended elementary school, people would assume that we already knew where I was going to college—that couldn't have been further from the truth. I am the perfect example of a true *discovery* college process. I flip-flopped about what I liked and disliked more times than I could count, and I learned more about myself with each college visit. Applying to Cornell Early Decision was decided only after an intense number of campus visits and careful thought.

> *As Amanda was deciding where to apply ED (she loved so many colleges), Cornell was not my first choice for her. When I insisted she "defend" her reasoning, in true Amanda form she presented many excellent reasons for making Cornell her ED choice.*

In order to better deal with friends, acquaintances, and peers throughout high school, I decided not to tell anyone about the following: my grade point average, standardized test scores, or college list (including my Early Decision school). In retrospect, it's not as if I am opposed to people knowing about my scores after the fact, but I kept this information to myself to avoid getting swept up in a competitive environment as much as possible. While the questions and occasional uncomfortable situations were inevitable, I am happy that I did not share my statistics while I was experiencing the process. I definitely did not need the additional stress of having people gossip about me.

I distinctly remember a moment in April of my junior year. I was in an elevator with an adult volunteering in school, a friend, and two other peers. As the adult asked each of us about our prospective colleges, he came to me and said, "What about you, Amanda? You totally know where you're going already, of course."

Amanda got questioned like this nearly everywhere she went. While I would like to think it was more helpful than not to have me as both a professional and a mom in this process, there is no doubt that the assumption that she already knew where she was going was a huge negative. Adults within our community would grill her whenever they saw the opportunity, even if they weren't friends with us or me.

While he was clearly half-kidding, this statement shook me a little. The truth is, I *didn't* know where I was going. I had to apply in the same way as everyone else. My mom may know a lot, but she isn't privy to some big secret. It was on that night that I decided I couldn't tell anyone my plans about where I was applying until it was over.

Here are some of the things I kept to myself, and my reasons for doing so.

GPA and Standardized Test Scores

Everyone in your class has a grade point average, and most everyone will have taken at least one SAT or ACT (if not a few of each) by the end of junior year. That's why they're called *college entrance exams*: people take them in order to be *Accepted* to college. While there are several amazing test-optional schools in the country, most people opt to at least *try* for a high score.

There are more than 950 test-optional colleges out there right now, which has freed many students from test-taking anxiety. Also, it is a financial savings when you do not have to prepare for, sit for, retake and submit testing. However, if you have the energy and resources to get to your best score, or if you are an athlete, I do recommend doing that. Good scores give you more options.

Regardless of testing, nearly every high school student in the world has a grade point average. Granted, not all GPAs are created equal (weighted/unweighted or including electives or not), but that's beside the point. Almost everyone has one.

You are most likely familiar with the braggers. These are the people who deliberately *go out of their way* to share their average and scores with you, and after doing so, <u>will ask to hear how you did.</u>

 And you should know that <u>sometimes they are not telling you the truth</u> anyway.

Don't get caught up in it—it's not worth it. By simply stating that you do not feel comfortable sharing, <u>people will slowly stop asking</u> you.

 Fantastic! And the more you tell people, <u>the more they get it</u>. I have had many students tell me that they wished they had done that throughout high school.

According to my standards, and compared to my practice test scores, I bombed my first ACT in December of my junior year. I remember how apprehensive I had felt about testing, and I worried that I was a "bad test-taker" who maybe would never reach my potential on a real exam. I was feeling okay about it until a girl volunteered how happy she was that she was finished with the ordeal because she had gotten a 34 (my dream score). That only made me feel worse, so when she asked me what I had scored, I told her that I was not comfortable sharing. I simply remarked, "I did fine, but I am taking it again."

Even if I had had a higher score at that point in the year, I wouldn't have told her—even if I had done better than she did. Regardless, I wouldn't ever give her the satisfaction of knowing my scores: they're my business, and my business only.

Why do I care? <u>I don't want my test scores to define me</u> as a person, good or bad. Sure, people know I'm fairly smart; I take challenging classes and participate in several extracurriculars, and I contribute to class discussions coherently (at least I think so). However, I know that the ACT is just one test and is not always *necessarily* a measure of my academic ability. In the midst of so many competitive classmates, I didn't really want people evaluating me based on a 36-point scale.

> *9* So true. Amanda would never tell you that she did, in fact, end up acing the ACT, but <u>it took months of grueling work and discipline</u> on her part to earn her score.

In addition to not sharing your own scores, it's probably best not to ask your friends and peers about theirs. Just <u>don't worry about other people</u>.

> *9* This is such a <u>good way to live</u> in general. ☺

I can tell you from experience that knowing how other people fared on their tests will only make you more anxious, and it definitely won't help you achieve your best possible score. When I started to hear rumors of what people had scored on their SATs and ACTs all throughout junior year, it made me either envious, surprised, mad, or pessimistic about my own results. I can't think of one incidence during which I felt good after knowing someone else's strong score. It's so much easier to keep these statistics to yourself, especially during high stakes testing periods in sophomore and junior years.

Enough Is Enough

Don't you feel as if you are forced to talk about school too much as it is? When you consider the time spent with your parents, teachers, and classmates while in school and/or studying, a lot of your high school life revolves around the classes you take. While it's understandable, normal, and healthy to discuss classes and teachers with your friends, there's no need for score comparison. Discussing your scores on a particular test won't help you do better on the next one. Also, you probably do have to discuss your grades with your parents occasionally. Do you really want to have another conversation about the hard test you took? It's not productive. Take a break from the anxiety and nervousness that often surrounds high schoolers in class, and just avoid the topic when hanging out with friends. Lessening the amount of time you spend talking about your scores will also decrease the chances that you're in an awkward position about sharing your scores.

In terms of college applications, believe me that they'll take up a great deal of your time at home. Everything takes longer than you expect it will. From composing emails to admissions counselors to writing six drafts of each essay to diligently answering every question on the Common App, this process will zap a lot of your time during the first few months of senior year. Plus, your visits and applications will probably be the subject of most family dinners. By the time you push *Submit* for the last time on each application, you will be pretty sick of the college talk and anxious for the decisions to arrive. Talking about your applications and college list with your friends will only make matters worse and more overwhelming. Use the time you have with them to your advantage (as a break) by simply not discussing college.

And When You Get to Senior Year...

Throughout the first several months of their senior year, most students will have college on the brain. As the year kicks into full swing, more and more people will log into Common App (or whatever application platform they are using), write their supplements, and finalize their lists. College becomes the number one topic of discussion, both in class and outside school.

In most schools (at least the ones I know about), the college "game" can get a bit competitive. Because students in the same high school tend to read about and apply to similar schools, the stakes are high when some people are *Accepted* to a particular school and others are not. This makes for awkward eye contact in class and an overall thickening of the air in school.

9 That makes me sad. The truth is, you are not only competing against people in your high school, but in your geographic region as well. The competition is not necessarily as direct as most students think it is.

I decided not to tell people where I was sending applications mainly because I did not want anyone knowing about my *Rejections*. It's not that I was concerned about their judgment, but instead that I knew I just wouldn't want to talk about it. It is *so* much easier to deal with *Rejection* if the whole world does not know about it.

The hardest secret to keep was where I applied Early Decision. To make matters worse, there were 11 students (that I knew about—probably a few more existed) who had also applied early to Cornell. While I knew that I would have been positively fine if I had not been *Accepted* ED to Cornell, and I would have been excited about other opportunities, I would have been really disappointed if *Rejected*.

9 This is my hope for all students: apply ED if you find a clear choice, but you must have other more *Likely School* options so you can be confident that you will get into a great college and be happy.

It was just easier if no one knew. As the Early Decision application deadline approached, I told everyone that I had applied early *somewhere*, but I did not want to jinx my chances by revealing the name of the school aloud. I was careful not to hint at Cornell, wear Cornell apparel, or even act too eager when the subject was brought up. While my good friends suspected I had applied there and everyone envisioned me fitting in well there, I did not confirm these beliefs until December 10, when the big news arrived in my email inbox.

If you decide not to tell anyone where you applied, don't underestimate how uncomfortable school will become. It will be *really* difficult to avoid the constant questioning and inevitable subject matter. However, it's worth it. If you don't get in, you won't have to deal with pity or with the condescension from students who did get in, for whatever reason.

Practically, sharing your grades, scores, or college lists will not be productive in any way. Resisting the temptation to get caught up in the drama and gossip will allow you to stay calm throughout an anxiety-producing process that lasts for several months—much longer if you get *Deferred* or *Waitlisted*. As long as you are confident in your actions and the decision not to share information, people will generally respect that and begin to leave you alone. You'll enjoy applying to college more if you're able to share only the exciting news at the end: where you'll end up.

Possible question	Possible response if you're "keeping your mouth shut"!
Where are you applying?	This is an easy one! Spit out a "fake list" of schools: colleges that would make sense for you, but that you are not applying to for whatever reason. Of course, you could also just be honest and say "my parents and I decided we will not be sharing this information."
What did you get on your ACT/SAT?	I did well. (But I'm taking it again. / I do not plan on taking it again.)
What's your first-choice college?	I love so many colleges, I don't have a first choice! (Hopefully, this is actually true.)
What's your GPA?	I prefer not to share. Sorry! (This is a fine response.)

CHAPTER 21

Parenting Throughout the Process

I remember the feeling well. Amanda was about to enter high school and I was about to be the mom of a high school student—*how did I get here already?* Of course, I always wear my "guidance counselor hat" when making decisions, but now I would have the added responsibility and honor to be a mom during Amanda's journey to college. It was exciting! As Amanda and I sat together in the high school's auditorium and listened to the guidance department and administrators give an overview about what to expect in the next four years, I looked around and saw lots of nervous faces. Parents and students alike seemed uneasy about high school. That's understandable, but I was ok. I was a school counselor, after all.

Having worked with hundreds—if not thousands—of students and their families for more than 20 years as they navigated the uncertainty of high school, I was eager now to be a mom in this journey. After thinking a lot about what kind of mom I wanted to be for Amanda during this process, I was certain that I wanted to be intentional about it. I wanted to think in advance about my role in this process and how I could help support my daughter throughout *her* high school journey. Despite people's perceptions of me, I did not have Amanda's experience all figured out. Many people assumed that I had already known where Amanda would go to college even before she started high school. I distinctly remember having a conversation with another mom who called me a liar when I wouldn't tell her what college Amanda would attend. Incredibly, even though Amanda and the woman's daughter were only in eighth grade at that point, this individual still insisted that she *knew* where her daughter would be going. Five years later, that's exactly the university she is attending. To me, this is sad. While I hope this girl is happy at her mother's college choice, I firmly believe that this needs to be the student's journey, not something predetermined by well-intentioned parents.

A few years ago, I had the pleasure and privilege of presenting a NACAC (National Association for College Admissions Counseling) webinar with Caroline Faris, a private high school counselor, to college counselors, public school counselors, and independent counselors across the country. Trying to be cute while getting my point across, I nicknamed the many different kinds of parents I have worked with in my practice.

> I think this concept is hilarious, but the descriptions about the different kinds of parents below are so true. I thought it was fun to try to assign each of my friends' parents one of the categories.

I do not think there is a right or wrong way to parent a teenager through high school because, obviously, your child's temperament, personality, academic, and personal interests will all play a huge role in the way parents might approach their roles in the child's high school career. If you are a parent and have a child in high school, you may get a kick out of reading my descriptions of the different "types" of parents with which I work and how they approach the college process with their children:

Silver Spoon parents do everything for their children. I have had these parents ask me to write essays for their children!

Ew. This is completely unfair. There are rumors in my school about parents like this, but I am not sure that they are actually true.

These are the overprotective parents whose intentions are usually good, but who have trouble letting go and allowing their children to take charge. For my Silver Spoon parents and their children, I usually suggest that they set aside a mutually convenient time each week to discuss college applications and/or academics. Only during this predetermined appointment slot are parents allowed to ask as many questions as they want and raise relevant concerns to discuss. The children, however, may bring up these topics to their parents at any point during the week. This helps to temper the parents' instinct to take over the process. It also enables the children to separate from their parents and remain in control of their journey.

It also helps to reduce the number of college conversations per week, which can get pretty overwhelming and tiring by the end.

Nervous Nellies are parents who are (surprise!) super nervous about high school, college, and the whole process in general.

One friend in particular comes to mind when I think of these parents. His mom is in overdrive all the time, and I think she drove my friend crazy during application season.

Of course, if you generally have a great deal of anxiety you will tend to be extra nervous throughout the college process. If you have access to Naviance (see Chapter 14 on *Using Common Application, Naviance, Universal Application, Coalition for Access and More*), it may be helpful to check the "admit rates" of the *Likely Schools* on your child's list. This will hopefully mitigate your anxiety and confirm that your child *will* get into college. I also suggest that Nervous Nellies talk through their worst fears with a trusted resource like the child's school counselor. One of Nervous Nellies' biggest worries is that their son or daughter will not get *Accepted* to any colleges. While many parents have expressed this concern to me, in my 20-plus years of guidance counseling this has never happened to any of my students. In fact, all of my students end up with at least three options. If you approach this process the right way and apply to enough *Likely Schools*, have no fear. However, let's say it does happen and your child gets *Rejected* from every school on his/her list—just for argument's sake. NACAC comes out with a list of hundreds of colleges that still have openings after May 1.

There are also numerous two-year community colleges, many with residence halls, which enroll most students with either a high school diploma or GED. Some universities have two-year college options within their institution. Also, remember that I suggest that students apply to at least one *Likely* option that is also a Rolling Decision school. Hopefully, your child will get an *Acceptance* under his/her belt early in senior year.

Go Harvard or Go Home parents believe that their child must attend an Ivy League institution.

A A lot of these parents exist in my town, which creates a very competitive, name-centered environment when it comes to applying and choosing colleges.

These parents need to educate themselves on the admit rates of the Ivy colleges and those of *Likely Schools* for their children; the odds of attending an Ivy are simply slim, no matter what your application looks like. Parents, if you fall into this category, I will assume that your child does exceptionally well in high school. You must understand that *most* Ivy applicants do extremely well in school— otherwise, why would they apply? High grades and high test scores will not differentiate your child. Remember that with thousands of colleges in America alone, surely there are several fantastic matches for your child that do not necessarily belong to the Ivy League. Embrace these options.

> **A** Believe it or not, although I ended up at Cornell, my mom was a huge proponent of my attending a small, liberal arts college with fewer undergraduates and smaller classes. There are so many unbelievable programs at small colleges not considered "top-tier" simply because of their names. However, don't let this deter you from applying; some are just as academically strong as Ivies. I applied to several of these schools and I know I would have been very lucky to attend one of them.

It is so important in this process for parents and children alike to be realistic about their chances at top-tier schools. Nothing is a guarantee in college admissions, and I believe that you are doing your children a disservice if you either subtly or overtly convey that their self-worth will in some way be tied to the name of the college they attend. If you look at the education histories of some of the finest and most successful people, many of them attended their state universities or less well-known schools. It is who you are as a person and what you do with your degree that matters.

Been There, Done That parents think they know everything, and tend to argue their way through most situations. Perhaps some parents have a good reason to know a lot about the college process; maybe they have already gone through this process with older children or a close friend. That's all great. However, let me tell you that even as a professional in the field, I learn something new almost daily. It amazes me how much the college process has evolved over the last two decades; I could never possibly know everything. Stay current and seek professional assistance when you need it. I think a good school counselor is a lot like a medical internist: you would likely not have a surgical procedure without a second opinion. School counselors need to know a lot, not only about the college process but also the high school details too. If your child attends a huge public high school where counselors do not have time to get to know the students, look elsewhere for help.

Here is a funny anecdote about my first day as a school counselor in Long Island, N.Y. I was 23 years old and probably looked as if I were still a student in high school myself. I began my career as a leave replacement for someone on maternity, so my first day of work was in February. A parent who had five children in my caseload made an appointment to meet me and she asked about 100 questions; I knew the answer to none of them. After writing down all her questions, I promised to find the answers from trusted resources like other school counselors and to get back to her before I left school for the day. Extremely irritated that the school had hired such a novice, that Been There, Done That mom immediately marched down to the principal's office after leaving me on the brink of tears. Thankfully, my wonderfully supportive principal called me to his office to assure me that this particular woman liked to "bust chops." For what it's worth, when *I* went on maternity leave many years later, this same woman did not want me to leave. She insisted that I stay to be her younger children's school counselor. The moral of this story is twofold. First, students, you need to believe in yourself and find a trusted adult who believes in you as well. Second, to the parents who think you know everything, you don't. No one does.

Smart and Sharp parents are well-educated and know plenty about the college process, but also <u>understand when to ask insightful questions</u> to further their knowledge. Good for you if you fall into this category.

 I'm lucky that <u>this is definitely my mom</u>. ☺

These parents have an informed consumer mentality. They do thorough and reliable research—not "I heard from my neighbor's aunt…"—and do not trust hearsay. They support their children but do not micromanage everything throughout the process.

Sink or Swim parents let their children find their way alone. Sometimes this is because both parents work full-time, take care of other children, or simply do not have time to devote to the college process. Sometimes it's because parents feel inadequate and/or are not educated themselves. These parents are probably not the ones reading this book. However, if you know a child who has parents like this, step in and offer some assistance. I'm a big believer that while the journey to college is also a journey to independence, teenagers still need lots of love, encouragement, and help at points along the way.

CHAPTER 22

Mulling the Future

Obtaining a college degree is a great thing. Your undergraduate years truly will encompass some of the best experiences in your life. And in the months leading up to college, thinking about where you want to live, how you want to live, and whom you want to meet should all be very exciting. Most likely, your family has made most of your important life decisions for you thus far. Your family likely decided where you would live and where you would attend high school. Suddenly, you find yourself on the brink of having to confront major changes because graduation could very well involve living with different people in an <u>unfamiliar locale for the next four years</u>. You get to choose where that is!

> Maybe everyone doesn't feel like this, but I get overwhelmed with excitement when I think about how much power I had in choosing a college, and then how much I can determine when I am at school. College is so different from high school. I think that <u>living away from home forces you to mature more quickly</u>.

While you may not get *Accepted* to every college you would like, if you follow the guidelines provided in this book and enjoy the journey, you will soon realize that there are literally dozens of schools that you would *love*. Don't even apply to one school that you do not love, as there is no reason for you to attend that school. This is why it is so crucial to have enough lovable *Likely Schools* on your list. Enjoy the application time as a way to learn more about yourself and your priorities, and embrace all that goes with it.

Then there is the other part of the future: <u>what happens after college?</u> You may have faced pressure and countless questions through the years about your intended major or career path.

A I always found it somewhat annoying when adults would ask me in high school what I was planning to choose as a career. My go-to answer was, "Well, I know what I *don't* want to do"— because that was true. For example, I never had interest in medical school or engineering. Besides that, while I know that I want to help people in some fashion, I really do not have one particular job in mind; I have had many that I would consider. I still don't know what I want to do, but I know that <u>I am excited to figure it out</u> and explore new things in college.

If you are anything like most high school students, <u>you likely do not have your future planned out yet</u>. This is okay and completely normal and healthy—do not let other people make you believe otherwise. Did you know that the average adult changes his/her career (not just job) anywhere from five to seven times?

A It is comforting to know that there are many adults who are still trying to figure out their lives. With that in mind, if I <u>start exploring options during college</u>, I'm ahead of the game, right?

If you consider that almost shocking statistic, understand that changing your major multiple times when you are in your late teens and early twenties in college is FINE.

I believe that your college experience is a time for finding opportunities, growth, and most importantly, yourself. Figure out what you like and what you do not, and absolutely do not put pressure on yourself to do this quickly—you have plenty of time. Truthfully, what makes me nervous is the high school student who come into my office in 10th or 11th grade with the attitude of "I have it all figured out." Do you really know already that you want to major in such and such and have a career in a specific field? Of course, there are the few exceptions: the students who have had a lifelong dream and go to college specifically to explore one thing.

> **A** Two friends come to mind: one friend who attends a specific university because she has always wanted to be an architect, and a friend who attends another school's seven-year medical program. Both friends only applied to very specific programs at colleges. I certainly do not have as clear an idea about my own future, but I guess all people are different, and if you have a lifelong dream, go get it! ☺

However, I think *all* students should allow for the possibility of change—even if you are sure you have figured your life out. No matter how much you think you know what you want to do as a career, because you are a teenager it is more than okay to figure it out as you go along. Take advantage of your college years as a time when you do not need to know your plan. Experiment by taking different kinds of classes, eating different kinds of foods, and trying different kinds of activities. Colleges try to create diversity for a reason: they want to expose you to the world.

There are many people who maintain that a college major needs to be in a job-related field. I could not disagree more with this opinion, and I have plenty of research behind me to make me feel this way. Consider the 2016 *New York Times* article "To Write Better Code, Read Virginia Woolf" to learn about the value of a liberal arts degree in pursuit of a STEM field. Students who know how to write well, think critically, and explain themselves articulately will get the jobs—almost regardless of what a major is called. Think about it: many first jobs require you to know very little about the actual tasks involved. The chances are that someone with more experience will teach you what you need to know. In almost all professions, <u>employers want to know that their new hires can think, analyze, and write</u>. A strong liberal arts degree will surely provide you with those skills.

 Mom, you are like a liberal arts cheerleader. She is a big fan of liberal arts. I also believe that writing and thinking critically are two of the most important life skills, but I think <u>you can get these from whatever and wherever you study</u> in college. There is absolutely no profession in which you won't have to write emails to bosses and coworkers or solve problems.

Employers prioritize liberal and applied learning for all college students, according to "Falling Short? College Learning and Career Success," a Hart Research Associates January 2015 study. They found that 91 percent of employers "agree that to achieve success at their companies, a candidate's demonstrated capacity to think critically, communicate clearly, and solve complex programs is more important than his or her undergraduate major…" To learn more about what you can do with a liberal arts education, please refer to LiberalArtsLife.org.

Many colleges allow students two years before they are required to declare a major, so <u>use the time beforehand to try new classes</u> and push yourself beyond what you thought was possible.

This time frame also depends on the university's rules and on the particular program.

Think of your freshman and sophomore years of college as time to figure things out and explore what makes you excited and enriched academically. Some schools allow students to take a few classes pass/fail instead of with grades that affect your GPA; if your college offers this option, you should <u>take these classes in areas</u>

outside your comfort zone. It is an amazing opportunity to learn new things without the added pressure of being graded.

 One of my favorite questions to ask tour guides when visiting colleges was, "Does the school have pass/fail classes?" I absolutely love the idea of taking classes in things that I have no experience in (computer science, for example), and getting to learn about the topic without having to worry about the grade. I remember when I first heard about this option from a Cornell tour guide in 10th grade and as a result started inquiring about pass/fail classes at all colleges.

However, do make sure that you still pay attention and attend those classes as well. I have seen students take a class pass/fail and then blow it off and almost not pass—clearly, that is not a great plan.

That's just silly. Why bother enrolling in the class?

If you want to push yourself, enroll in the class and actively engage in the assignments and reading. You will have two great outcomes: first, you learned about something new and decided whether you like it (both reactions are equally valuable). Second, you did not have to worry about getting a good grade but yet you were still engaged during the semester to accomplish more than the minimum requirements.

At some colleges, you can also get special titles next to your degree if you take extra electives or complete minors or concentrations. College is definitely not all about one major.

The biggest exceptions regarding choosing a major are in the fields of engineering and architecture. Because there are so many requirements for both fields, if you are leaning toward one of these areas, it is a good idea to start fulfilling class criteria and credits with your college's major as soon as possible. You may decide that these fields are not for you and switch into something else with little concern. However, if you start in another major and later decide to switch to engineering or architecture, you will likely be in college substantially longer than four years. This is not a huge deal, but it is certainly worth consideration from a time and financial perspective.

In the past, I told students that it was totally okay to be *Undecided* when actually applying to college. Now, with so many more applicants than ever, I think that it is more difficult for admissions counselors to admit students who are *Undecided*. This is simply because it is more challenging to determine which majors will fill up if too many students do not specify a major when they apply. Alternatively, rather than declaring *Undecided*, you can indicate two or three subjects in which you are currently most interested. While it is 100% okay not to know what you want to major in or do for a career, I do think you should indicate something just to put yourself into a category for admissions purposes.

A My thinking is that if there's no harm in declaring a major and you can always change your mind, it's an opportunity to explore an interest, at the very least.

When deciding what major to check, study your high school transcript and extracurricular activities. How do you spend your time? I recently had a student who indicated that she wanted to major in Religious Studies, but the truth is, she was not totally sure. However, she was attending parochial school, spent summers at a religious camp took several religious classes, and studied the Bible. Majoring in Religious Studies was more a choice of interest—she was not certain if it would be her ultimate major. By examining her transcript and activities, though, a college will understand the reasoning behind her intended major and be able to put her into the "Religious Studies box."

No matter what path you choose, seek help from advisors, professors, older friends, mentors, and your college's career services program. Listen to all the advice you receive and choose to do what works best for you. Interning, volunteering, and/or working in fields of interest during college are educational experiences that sometimes lead to fascinating opportunities beyond college. Do not take any of this all too seriously—remember the statistic about adults changing their minds. Also, don't forget the saying, *if you find something you love to do, you won't ever work a day in your life.*

A Although I am not an adult yet, <u>I know from my mom's example that this is true.</u> She loves working with students as a private guidance counselor (and talks even more fondly of her school guidance counselor days). My primary goal for my career is to find something I love so much that it does not feel like work.

Your job and career are really whatever you make them to be. I would encourage you to read Frank Bruni's *New York Times* article "How to Survive the College Admissions Madness" from March 2015 and/or his book about this topic: *Where You Go Is Not Who You'll Be: An Antidote to the College Admissions Mania.*

CHAPTER 23

Keeping the Proper Perspective

Whether you attend Harvard, your local community college, or any school between them, you will learn new things, meet new people, and expand your horizons. What you do with the experiences at any institution will be enormously fulfilling—if you take advantage of the resources offered. Although attending a school such as Harvard has a certain cachet and bumper sticker appeal, there is more that matters in a college education. There's no doubt that graduating from a prestigious university will help you land your first job and/or get into graduate school. However, there are literally thousands of other schools that produce very successful people. I firmly believe—with the support of extensive research—that where you spend your years as an undergraduate will have anywhere from zero to little impact on your life 20 years after graduation.

Just as you should not let one bad test grade or one mistake define your life, you should not let the name of a school define you. In fact, *you* can define the *school* by accomplishing amazing things, both while you are a student and after graduation.

If you are still bothered by a particular instance in your life when you felt deflated by something that a mentor or teacher said or did, consider these facts:

- ▶ Thomas Edison, the famous inventor of the electric light bulb, was considered mentally ill as a child and was told by his teachers that he could not learn.
- ▶ Louis Pasteur, the famous French scientist, received a grade of "mediocre" in chemistry in college.
- ▶ Louisa May Alcott, the author of the classic *Little Women*, was told by an editor that she could never write anything that would sell.
- ▶ J.K. Rowling was turned down by 12 publishers before her *Harry Potter* series was published.
- ▶ Ludwig van Beethoven, the great composer, was called "hopeless" as a composer by one of his music teachers.
- ▶ Albert Einstein, the brilliant scientist, did not learn to speak until age four or read until age seven. One teacher called him "retarded."
- ▶ Walt Disney was fired by a newspaper editor who said Disney had "no good ideas."

Amanda's Perspective

If you think about all the older kids you know who are currently in college, are any of them unhappy? Probably not—and if they are, they have a plan to transfer. The truth is that most people learn to fall in love with their schools because making friends and memories for the rest of your life will result regardless of where you end up. The location almost does not matter. When you return to visit your high school as a college freshman, remember that you will be bursting to share all your amazing experiences thus far. At my school, college freshmen attend an Alumni Brunch the day before Thanksgiving break, and the main hall is swarming with students eager to talk about how much they love their schools. If you do not get *Accepted* to your top school, embrace the opportunity to go to a school that is slightly below your academic ability—maybe you'll receive a helpful merit scholarship or enjoy feeling smarter than most of your classmates.

I know my credibility in this field is somewhat diminished because I applied to Cornell Early Decision and got in. However, I swear that if I had not been admitted, while I would have been upset, <u>I would have been thrilled to investigate my other options</u>.

J This is true! The day before Amanda heard from Cornell, she said, "I know that I'll be happy wherever I end up at school. I'd love to go to Cornell and have this process behind me so I can enjoy the rest of high school and learning, and not worry too much about grades." Amanda *loves* her AP classes and learning. This is wonderful and certainly a perk about Early Decision: the ability to truly enjoy school without the pressure of grades. A great takeaway here is that because <u>she had so many colleges on her list</u> that she visited and loved, she knew she would end up in a great school.

When the Cornell decisions were released, I had already been *Accepted* into the Honors Program of a state school I adored.

One of my camp friends applied Early Decision to a top liberal arts school and was *Rejected*. What made this especially hard is that we knew of other kids in my grade who were *Accepted*. On the night she found out, I took her out to sushi and FroYo and listened to her cry over the loss of her first-choice school. I gave her the advice that any good friend would suggest: you have so many other schools; don't let this define you; you will be so happy wherever you end up. At the time, she was devastated, understandably. However, in less than two weeks, she got into another great school in the Early Action round, and committed there almost right away. Even a month after she heard from the ED school, she was already connected with her new roommate and was sporting clothes to showcase her chosen university. I am so proud of her that she let her first choice go and recognized that she would be equally happy at another college.

CHAPTER 24

Knowing What I Did Right

Hey, everyone. Amanda here. While I made plenty of mistakes throughout the college application process, I did do a lot of things right. I wanted to dedicate this chapter to a list of my general suggestions that hopefully will make the college application journey less daunting.

We have not exactly kept it a secret that grades count in high school. They do. When you do badly on a test (assuming this is out of character for you), always talk to your teacher. Don't whine and attempt to gain back points; just try to articulate why you bombed. Although it's unlikely that teachers will change your grade as a result of the conversation, that's not the point. Hopefully, <u>your teacher will learn how to best help you achieve a better score</u> on your next assessment.

> *And remember that <u>one test in one class does not amount to much at the end</u>. You will likely bomb a few tests along the way—you can still finish with a strong GPA.

This goes without saying, but work as hard as you can. <u>Give 100% effort</u> to every assignment and you will almost never let yourself down.

While that is admirable, <u>I'm not sure it's always realistic.</u> There are plenty of other life factors (illness, death in the family) and extracurricular activities that could interfere with this goal. That's ok, that's life. If you prioritize your academics as much as you can, it should be fine.

Despite tests, try as best as you can to enjoy school—<u>enjoy learning</u>. Enjoy the feeling of information seeping into your brain. The clock will move a lot faster.

<u>Yes!</u>

<u>Don't procrastinate</u>, as tempting as it may seem. Whether it's homework, long-term assignments, or college applications, just get the work done as soon as possible.

<u>Good time management is a great skill</u>, both in high school and in life.

If your high school allows you to modify your schedule prior to the start of classes, always prioritize getting good teachers over getting classes with friends. School is for learning; if your friends happen to end up in your classes, that's a huge bonus. You will be happier in the long-run if you get the best teachers possible for each subject.

If you are lucky enough to have more than one free period in a day, spend one of them studying or starting your homework. <u>Allow yourself one period</u> a day to chill, hang with friends, eat, and so on.

Yes! There is often the temptation to take as many classes as you can possibly fit into your schedule, but having <u>down time is super important</u> for your mental health.

Keep Your Mouth Shut (See Chapter 20).

If you are able to qualify financially and academically, apply Early Decision to your first choice. If you get in, the rest of senior year will be a breeze.

 Statistically speaking, there is a significant advantage to getting in through Early Decision. However, please read about ED before signing such a binding contract. This plan is not for most students. You need to have visited lots of other colleges and be able to articulate why a specific school is your absolute number one choice. And, you cannot just disregard the rest of high school. If you are *admitted*, your ED college will expect that you will finish high school with about the same grades as when you applied. The pressure may be off, but there is still a certain level of responsibility.

Apply Early Action to all schools that have this option.

Visit as many *Likely Schools* as possible to ease your stress. If you know (or are pretty sure) that you will get *Accepted* to a school that you love, you'll feel as if a huge weight has been lifted from your chest. I promise.

This was one of the best things that we did, for sure.

CHAPTER 25

What I Wish I Had Done Differently

Thankfully, I do not have many regrets about high school. However, there are a few things that I do wish I had done differently, or would do differently if I could start over in ninth grade. I divided my points into two categories: what I wish I did differently in high school, and then specifically what actions during the college process would I alter. I also interviewed some friends to see if they had any regrets, and included some of their responses in my notes.

In High School

I wish I had explored chorus. I had stopped in middle school because I could only take one music class and, at the time, I chose band. When I eventually dropped band, <u>I should have picked up chorus</u> because I like to sing. Oh, well.

> *J* At least you participated in the school musicals to enjoy a little singing. And, don't forget, <u>Cornell has lots of singing opportunities</u>, in case you want to pursue them.

I'm not sure that there was actually enough time in my schedule before senior year, but I wish I had started tutoring earlier. It is such an easy and enjoyable way to make money and to help children at the same time. I can only imagine how cool it would have been to develop long-lasting relationships with younger kids throughout all four years of high school.

Here is my biggest piece of advice to my younger self: <u>do not worry about each and every little grade</u>. Of course, try your best, but there's no need to get angry if you do not do well once in a while. Not only will grades even themselves out, but also if you have fair teachers, your course grades should truly reflect your overall capability in any class. I have failed tests before, but I'm still here and thriving. Bad grades are not the end of the world. Of course, some students' parents need to get that memo.

 Amanda, <u>I hope you will carry this advice</u> through with you to college.

Throughout the College Process

My friends who procrastinated all said they wished that they had started writing their essays earlier. No one wants to be stuck at home on Halloween night, cramming to submit applications on November 1 to schools with early deadlines. <u>Get a jumpstart during the summer</u> so you can enjoy the fall.

 Amanda was away for almost the entire summer before her senior year. During the two weeks between camp ending and school starting, she literally worked all day on her applications. She wrote essay after essay, and was beyond diligent. The end result was that <u>before school started in September, she was 90% done with her application process</u>. Amanda wanted to take part in the fall high school musical (which demands a crazy amount of time). She knew her applications had to be almost completed in order to fully enjoy participating in the musical. Organization is key!

I wish I had used Google Docs and Drive more than I did. The system is so helpful and is free, and I would have saved storage space on my computer.

One friend told me that she wished she had never told anyone her SAT score. She said, "I hated how my friends would assign me to a certain level of school based on my score."

I wish I had taken all my standardized tests at other high schools. I only did this at the end of junior year, but I learned that I absolutely loved not knowing anyone. If no one knows you, <u>no one bothers you</u>.

𝓰 This is good to know because I think most people are upset if they don't get assigned their home schools for standardized tests.

CHAPTER 26

Tips for Incoming First-Year College Students

The end of your senior year of high school can be both exciting and overwhelming. To assist you in making a positive adjustment to college life, I want to offer you the following information based on ideas that my former students have shared with me.

First of all, did you know that research studies indicate 78% of all first-year college students experience feelings of anxiety, homesickness, and loneliness during the first six weeks of school? No matter how "cool" most of your fellow freshmen appear to be, remember this statistic. Remember that you are not alone.

Tips

▶ For 18 years, adults have been around to warn you of potential consequences of any poor decisions you might make. When you leave home, it is highly unlikely that anyone will assume that role. "Play it safe" academically for the first six weeks. Make daily and weekly schedules of what you plan to accomplish, and stick to them. Study for two or three hours per every hour spent in class or lectures. Studies show that if you have an organized work plan, your chances of success increase. You can modify your schedule after you receive mid-semester grades.

▶ As soon as you arrive on campus, find out how to drop or add a class. What is the deadline for dropping a class? Do you need an advisor's signature prior to making schedule changes? These are critical questions. Many students need to adjust their first-semester schedules of their freshman year. If you can, initially sign up for one "extra" class with the intention of eventually dropping one. This will give you the flexibility to determine which classes will work best for you.

▶ At least for the first six weeks of school, do not eat alone. Instead, if you do not have plans with friends, seek out other people who are sitting by themselves. You can learn a lot from meeting other random students on campus, and you will definitely feel less lonely. Some freshmen have met so many people this way that they end up running for freshmen political positions in student groups—and often winning.

▶ Establish some rules or guidelines with your roommate *before* you get to know each other, preferably on the first or second day. Discuss quiet hours, boyfriends/girlfriends in the room, and so on. If you already know your roommate through social media, you can set up some guidelines when you speak before school begins. Your goal with your roommate should be to live well together. If you become best buds, that's a bonus.

▶ Find out about health services at your school at the very beginning of the semester—before you need them. Where is the health center? What are its hours? Any cost? If you get sick first semester, it can make you homesick as well. If you're prepared, you can be well-equipped to take care of yourself. You may want to keep some over-the-counter medications available in your room so you don't have to run to the drugstore or health center if you just need a Tylenol.

▶ Before you leave home, make sure everyone in the family knows who is paying for what expenses, such as textbooks and weekend trips. This helps you and your parents to budget funds.

▶ If you want a checking account, open one at the college business office or at a local bank. If your parents are contributing to your spending money, give them deposit slips so they can put money into your account. Pay all your bills by check and write reasons for the expenditures on the check. This will serve as a receipt for payment plus a yearly record of expenses. If you will be using a credit card, be sure to pay your bills on time and in full every month. Lastly, don't forget to check your statements each month for accuracy (this can be done online).

▶ Sign all documents with your first name, middle initial and last name. Because you are registered in your given name, you should avoid using nicknames.

▶ Identify support systems before you leave home. If you are feeling low, do you play the guitar, hit the gym, or attend religious services? Take your support systems with you to college by getting involved in intramural sports or which-ever activities calm you. In college, you can still sing in the shower. Wear your favorite baseball cap. Keep a beloved stuffed animal from childhood on your bed.

▶ You should find out about the athletic facilities on your campus and/or in neighboring communities. Exercising will help you feel good on a regular basis, and it will provide an additional way to meet people.

▶ Don't bring your car to school for your first semester, even if you are allowed. Everyone wants to feel popular, but when you have a car you will be used. You will feel guilty if you say "no" when someone wants to borrow your car or when you need to study but your friends want you to drive them to get pizza instead. There is pressure involved with having a car on campus, so if you take yours to college have your policies prepared for the first time someone approaches you about being the chauffeur.

▶ Save $250 before you leave for college. This emergency fund can assist with unexpected costs such as the deposit for a lost room key or an unexpected textbook purchase.

▶ If you are receiving financial aid and your package includes a work-study, I recommend that as soon as you are paid, you immediately endorse your paycheck and give it to the business office. Ask the office to apply it to your account, which will ensure that you won't get caught short for second semester. You must work the hours you are assigned if you have a work-study plan. Work-study earnings are considered an essential component to funding your college education by the financial aid process.

▶ Professors are available for discussing class materials and other concerns. Find out when they will be in their offices and get to know them both as teachers and people. The instructors will usually provide their office number and office hours on the first day of class.

▶ Find out what tutoring facilities are available on campus. Use them if you need them—or even before you need them—as soon as you find yourself falling behind and not understanding something your professor is covering.

Before you go to college, imagine that you get Ds. What is the contingency plan? Don't start school until you know exactly what you will do if your classes are more difficult than you had expected.

▶ Watch yourself for excess in any behavior. Examples include apathy, all work and no play, changes in your sleep patterns such as insomnia or too much sleep, and eating too much or too little. Check to see if you're doing too much of anything, such as either constant partying or staying in your room. Seek out other people and talk about your issues. Go immediately to your R.A., a close friend, or some other trusted person on campus if something is wrong. Everyone who moves into a new adventure, like attending college, will experience some feelings of self-doubt or fear of failure.

▶ Keep in mind that date rape occurs most often during the first semester of freshman year, and most cases involve excessive drinking. Take precautions. Make sure that at least one person or friend (like a roommate) knows beforehand what time you expect to return to your dorm and where you are going. When you go out with a group, make a rule that you will all return together. Never walk alone at night.

▶ When you get to school, handwrite your parents a letter thanking them for sending you to school. It is an easy thing to do and will mean a great deal to them.

▶ When you go home for a school break, remember that your younger siblings and other relatives likely idolize you. You are a role model; be a positive one.

▶ Ask your parents not to remodel your bedroom during your first year of college. They may not understand your reasoning, but when you come home it will be comforting for you to live in exactly the same room you had left.

During the Summer Before College...

▶ Read at least three challenging books (at least one nonfiction). College demands that students are readers, and reading is a skill you will need for your entire life. It's also a great idea to read a few issues of your college's newspaper. Because it will mention important people and specific activities, you'll learn a lot about campus life before actually starting your freshman year.

▶ Watch movies and television in your chosen foreign language. Take placement tests or challenging language classes when you arrive on campus.

▶ Strengthen your math skills if necessary. You can take an online high school course, visit the Khan Academy website (khanacademy.org) for specific math questions, or check out the videos at Brightstorm.com.

▶ Don't live like a vampire. Wake up before 9 a.m. and get 8–10 hours of sleep. Eat a high protein breakfast and increase your vegetable intake. Healthful eating and sleeping habits during the summer will train you for the rigors of college.

▶ Exercise at least three days a week. You have more leisure time during the summer, so don't just sit around.

▶ Visit the career center during your first week on campus before classes start to find out the dates of the first internship or job fair. It can be as early as September or October. This gives staff an opportunity to know you as someone with his/her "lights on."

CHAPTER 27

Amanda's Archive
(Amanda's Common App Essay
and Sample "*Why*" Supplement)

If you are completely lost about essay writing, we thought we would help you out a bit by showing you some of Amanda's work. In this section, we included her Common App essay and one sample "*Why*" supplement. Enjoy!

Question: Discuss an accomplishment or event, formal or informal, that marked your transition from childhood to adulthood within your culture, community, or family.
Word limit: 650. Words: 643

"I got this one," I say to my co-counselor, preparing for a familiar battle of wills. But in just a few seconds, my camper Bailey had covered a lot of ground. My feet follow the pigtails and tie dye shorts as a basketball whizzes inches away from my head and I dodge the outfielders of a softball game.

"Bailey!" I yell, though it's no use—she's already making her way across the pond and heading toward the hills of the Adirondack Mountains. This is already her third tantrum of the hour and likely the thirtieth of the day, yet I have no choice but to trudge after her through the murky water.

One minute and two waterlogged sneakers later, I catch up to Bailey and sit down beside her. Her chapped fingernails are digging a hole in the soft earth, her mouth setting into a pout, her wild blue eyes furrowing into a glare.

As much as I want to help this kid, I'm rapidly losing patience. *Here we go again.*

She doesn't even give me enough time to strategize an opening statement. "They're all cheaters at kickball," she announces.

I look toward the mountains for some inspiration and I decide to try something new. Instead of attempting to convince her that so-and-so did not cheat, I choose to ask Bailey a very basic question. "Why did you come to camp this summer?"

She is obviously surprised by my question, and although I see that she's trying to be disagreeable, she considers it.

"Because I want to be in a place where no one thinks I'm a monster."

"A *what*?"

"A monster," she says, now softly. "That's what everyone calls me at home."

We sit in silence, her words lingering as I try to understand what Bailey is going through.

Suddenly, my heart drops through my stomach and rolls down the mountain. I'm transported back to a time in seventh grade when some girls at school decided to pick on me. Unstructured periods during the day were my worst nightmare, and for a few months I had no confidence. Everything turned out fine for me after those few challenging months at school, but my camp friends stuck with me through it all. Since I was just ten years old, they were the people I trusted without hesitation, the people I laughed with the hardest, the people I cried with the most—and all without judgment. Each summer, I return because camp brings out the best in me, and has helped shape the person I am today.

As my mind returns to the moment, I realize that Bailey is in camp to escape her own nightmare at home. Camp gives her the opportunity to start again, make friends, and create a safe haven for herself. Somehow, someway, I have to help Bailey adjust to camp. I was once a little girl at camp like Bailey and this is my chance to pay it back—now *I'm* the confident one; *I'm* the adult. I have the power to help her, and I will. Camp shouldn't just be for the "easy" kids—more than anyone else, Bailey needs a place to be loved and supported. If Bailey's tantrums are going to require 80 percent of my attention in a given day, so be it. If she refuses to get out of bed, fine. I have to do whatever it takes to make camp work for Bailey. Never again will I get frustrated with her melodrama. I have to view her as a work in progress, a kid who has potential and just needs to reach it.

With a shift in attitude and heart, I tilt her head upwards, look her in the eye, gently remove her hands from the dirt, and say, "Then let's go back. At camp you can be whoever you want to be."

• • •

What are the unique qualities of our university—and of the specific undergraduate school(s) to which you are applying— that make you want to attend the university? In what ways do you hope to take advantage of the qualities you have identified? *Word Limit: 300. Words: 251*

"X is *the* perfect school," I told my dad, as we toured the campus in 2013. Though I was only a rising sophomore, I loved X then, and I love it even more now. An admissions counselor, Amy Winnick, even calls me a "super-fan," as I attended a senior information meeting as a junior, as well as five additional sessions throughout high school.

My desire to emphasize creative writing drives my interest in applying to the College of Arts and Sciences. Having completed a Creative Writing Independent Study in high school, I'm especially excited about the prospect of taking the *Full Year Writing Sequence* in fiction or nonfiction, or *The Varieties of Writing* class where I'd be able to continue my study of a writer's influences. I would seek to supplement my English coursework in the School of Journalism with foundational classes such as *Modern Journalism*. I've written for my school newspaper, *The Southerner*, since ninth grade and would work hard to earn a position as a writer for *The Weekly*.

I would also be eager to join the Neighborhood Kids club to blend my interests in helping others and interacting with children. I have had a great deal of practice in both areas through my extensive involvement in Key Club, my job as a sleep-away camp counselor for eight-year-olds, and my teaching position at religious school.

With its contagious red spirit and ideal fields of study, not to mention its beautiful suburban location, X is a great match for me.

Epilogue

Hi everyone, it's Amanda. I have just completed my first semester as a freshman at Cornell, and I loved every minute of it. I wanted to share something I wrote for one of Cornell's literary magazines, Slope Media: "An Open Letter to My Childhood Friends." (*Originally appeared in the Fall 2016 issue of *Slope Magazine*. Reprinted with permission.)

I may be at college now living far away from you, the people with whom I grew up, but some things never change. You are still the first people I call when I'm tired, happy, or just need to rant about studying; you are still the ones I text when something embarrassing happens at school and I need to disappear into my phone; you are still the ones who know me the best since you remained by my side throughout all of my awkward phases—including my years of braces.

What's weird now is that you don't know the ins and outs of my life like you did in high school. Sure, on the phone I've told you my friends' names, where they are from, and what I did on the particular day that I called you. What I can't do is text you that so-and-so (a new friend) asked me such-and-such (a big favor), and for you to know exactly the dynamic of that conversation.

What's equally weird is that it's the same the other way around. I don't know the names of your five classes and teachers, the somewhat flirty conversation you had with that guy in your Chemistry discussion section, or what you talked about at the pizza place at 3 a.m. on Saturday night with your three best friends. I don't know your favorite study spot, dining hall, or club, not because they aren't important to you but because during our limited time to speak, you want to tell me stories about other more pressing items.

With time, after long breaks where we reunite in our home town, spending the days driving around and visiting our favorite restaurants, I'm sure I'll slowly get to know and understand this new chapter in your life. I want to hear about the craziest thing your roommate said and the topic of the hardest test you have taken this semester. I want to know the personalities of each friend in your dorm and how everyone else's backgrounds landed them at the same college you eventually chose.

I don't talk to you every day, and sometimes not even every week, but I do think about you more than you know. I care deeply about our relationships and your lives, and I'm constantly reminded through texting, Snapchat, Instagram, and the occasional phone call that we do still have so much in common despite living so far apart.

We all started new journeys just a few short months ago. They pulled each of us to all different states and countries, towns and cities, teachers, friends, and acquaintances. We are living—and thriving—in totally new worlds surrounded by new people, places and ideas we had never imagined. However, our personalities have not changed, and I know our reunions will feel as if we never left. When we go home, our conversation will be filled with exchanges such as "I'm not surprised" and "of course you did that." You know the girl I was, am, and will be forever, yet I can tell you how my aspirations have changed regarding the person I want to become one day.

Even when I am too busy to have an hour-long conversation with you, I love you and I miss you. I know you are my friends forever; I cannot wait to introduce you to the new world and niches I recently created for myself; and I cannot wait to hear about yours.

What I've begun to realize is this: you are my friends from childhood—high school, camp, extracurricular activities—and though I've made many good friends in a new environment I call home, no one can replace you. All the close friends I've made throughout my life thus far who are still in touch with my daily life are my "forever friends"—one group of people. It doesn't matter whether you came into my life when I was 8 or 18; what matters is that you have not left it.

About the Authors

Jill Madenberg has worked in the college admissions field since 1993 as a high school guidance counselor, college admissions representative, and independent college consultant. She loves to demystify the college process for students and their parents and ease their anxiety, encouraging them to embrace the journey together. Jill speaks regularly to students and their families about the college admissions process and has conducted seminars for other professionals learning about the college process. She has visited hundreds of college campuses during her career. In her private practice, Jill works closely with students to identify potential colleges, plan course selection and testing strategies, develop essay ideas, and manage the application process. Jill's counseling philosophy is that of supporting students and their families to explore options, maximize fit, maintain sanity, and enable success.

Jill is a longtime member of the Independent Educational Consultants Association, Higher Education Consultants Association and the National Association for College Admissions Counselors, and was trained at the Harvard Summer Institute on College Admissions. Jill earned her master's degree in counseling and guidance Summa Cum Laude from New York University and a bachelor's degree from The George Washington University. She has been interviewed for articles in *The New York Times* and *USA Today*, and for features on National Public Radio and Fox News.

• • •

Amanda Madenberg coauthored this book as a graduating senior from Great Neck South High School on Long Island, New York, before attending Cornell University. She is majoring in Human Development and hopes to pursue a career in the education or counseling fields. Amanda has worked with children in many capacities, including as a religious school teacher, camp counselor, babysitter, and mentor. She has also been active in numerous school and community service organizations. Reading and writing are two of Amanda's favorite pastimes, and she continues to write for school publications and just for fun.

Index